Chapter 1: The Real Political Financial Lobbies or Populism

The Influence of Corporate Lobbies on Democratic Decision-Making

Corporate lobbies can have a significant influence on democratic decision-making by utilizing their financial resources and political connections to shape policies and legislation in their favor. These lobbyists often represent the interests of large corporations and industries, seeking to influence lawmakers and government officials to support policies that benefit their clients.

One way in which corporate lobbies can influence democratic decision-making is through campaign contributions and financial support for political candidates. By donating money to political campaigns, lobbyists can gain access to lawmakers and influence their decisions on important issues. This can create a conflict of interest for politicians who may feel indebted to these corporate interests.

In addition to financial support, corporate lobbies also engage in extensive lobbying efforts to persuade lawmakers to support their positions on various issues. This can involve meeting with lawmakers, providing them with research and information to support their arguments, and mobilizing grassroots support for their cause. These lobbying efforts can be highly effective in swaying lawmakers to support policies that benefit corporate interests.

Furthermore, corporate lobbies often have close relationships with government officials and regulatory agencies, allowing them to have a direct influence on the decision-making process. This can result in policies that favor corporate interests over the interests of the general public or other stakeholders.

Overall, the influence of corporate lobbies on democratic decision-making can undermine the principles of fairness and equality in the political process. It is important for lawmakers and government officials to be transparent about their interactions with corporate lobbyists and to prioritize the needs and interests of the public when making policy decisions.

So the influence of corporate lobbies on democratic decision-making has become an urgent concern for those who hold dear the principles of true democracy! Let's dive deep into the intricate interplay between corporate interests and democratic processes, illuminating the ways in which these mighty entities can shape the destiny of our democracy!

In a system that heavily depends on substantial financial resources for political campaigns and elections, these corporate interests wield considerable power by strategically aligning themselves with candidates and parties that further their own agendas. Consequently, the fairness and integrity of democratic processes are called into question, as the voices of ordinary citizens are easily overshadowed by the deep pockets of these influential corporate actors!

The pervasive influence exerted by corporate lobbies on democratic decision-making undeniably jeopardizes the very essence of genuine democracy. The alarming dominance of financial prowess in politics, coupled with the surge of populism and the manipulative role played by media, collectively conspire to mold the outcomes of democratic processes. In order to fiercely protect the integrity of our cherished democracy, it becomes imperative for citizens, policymakers, and media organizations to ardently partake in a discerning examination of these intricate dynamics, and diligently strive towards forging a political system that is both fair and transparent.

Understanding Corporate Lobbies and their Objectives

Corporate lobbies have become an integral part of modern democratic societies, exerting significant influence on political decision-making processes. In this subchapter, we aim to delve into the inner workings of these corporate lobbies, their objectives, and the impact they have on democratic systems.

In a real democracy, the power dynamics between political financial lobbies and populism play a crucial role. It is essential to understand how these lobbies operate and the objectives they seek to achieve. Corporate lobbies, often representing the interests of big businesses and wealthy individuals, aim to shape policies and regulations in their favor. Through strategic lobbying efforts, they seek to influence lawmakers and governments to pass legislation that aligns with their economic interests. This raises questions about the true representation of the people's will and the extent to which corporate power distorts democratic decision-making.

Listed below are 20 goals of corporate lobbyists:

1. Shape government policies and regulations to benefit the corporate sector.

2. Defend and advance the interests of their member companies.

3. Secure advantageous tax policies and incentives for corporations.

4. Lobby for deregulation and decreased government oversight in industries.

5. Oppose regulations that could impact corporate profits negatively.

6. Advocate for trade agreements that serve their members.

7. Influence legislation concerning labor rights and workplace rules.

8. Push for laws that safeguard intellectual property rights.

9. Advocate for energy policies favorable to their industries.

10. Lobby for funding and backing for research and development in their sectors.

11. Shape public opinion on industry-related matters.

12. Advocate for policies that enhance economic growth and stability.

13. Support political candidates who share their interests.

14. Oppose policies that might increase costs for their members.

15. Promote corporate social responsibility initiatives to enhance their reputation.

16. Lobby for government contracts and procurement opportunities for their members.

17. Influence international trade policies for the benefit of their industries.

18. Advocate for access to foreign markets for their member companies.

19. Support policies that encourage innovation and entrepreneurship in their sectors.

20. Lobby for infrastructure investments that benefit their industries.

The influence of corporate lobbies on democratic decision-making is immense. With their vast financial resources, these lobbies can fund political campaigns, sway public opinion through media campaigns, and gain access to influential policymakers. By doing so, they can shape the political landscape and push their preferred policies, often at the expense of the broader public interest. Understanding the mechanisms through which corporate lobbies exert their influence is crucial in safeguarding the democratic process.

Examining the Relationship between Corporate Lobbies and Politicians

Corporate lobbying is a common practice in many countries, where businesses and industries seek to influence government decision-making in their favor. This can take the form of providing financial support to political campaigns, hiring lobbyists to advocate on their behalf, or offering other forms of incentives to politicians.

The relationship between corporate lobbies and politicians can be complex and controversial. On one hand, corporate lobbying can be seen as a legitimate way for businesses to voice their concerns and advocate for policies that benefit their interests. It can also provide valuable expertise and information to policymakers, helping them make more informed decisions.

However, there are also concerns about the influence that corporate lobbies can have on politicians and the political process. Critics argue that corporate interests can distort policymaking, leading to decisions that primarily benefit wealthy corporations rather than the broader public interest. There are also concerns about the potential for corruption, with politicians being swayed by financial contributions or other incentives from corporate lobbyists.

To address these concerns, many countries have implemented regulations and disclosure requirements for corporate lobbying activities. These measures are intended to increase transparency and accountability in the relationship between corporate lobbies and politicians, ensuring that decisions are made in the public interest rather than for the benefit of a select few.

Overall, the relationship between corporate lobbies and politicians is a complex and nuanced issue that requires careful consideration and oversight to ensure that it serves the public good rather than the interests of a wealthy few.

In the realm of modern democracy, it is crucial to understand the complex and often contentious relationship between corporate lobbies and politicians. Here we delves into the intricate dynamics that exist between these two entities, highlighting the significant influence of corporate lobbies on democratic decision-making and the detrimental impact of money in politics. It is imperative to recognize and address these issues to uphold the integrity of our democratic processes.

Analyzing the Impact of Corporate Lobbies on Policy Formation

Corporate lobbies play a significant role in shaping policy formation by influencing decision-makers and advocating for policies that align with their interests. These lobbies represent the interests of large corporations and industries, often using their financial resources and connections to push for policies that benefit their members.

One impact of corporate lobbies on policy formation is the potential for bias in decision-making. Lobbies may prioritize the interests of their members over the needs of the general public, leading to policies that benefit corporations at the expense of consumers or the environment. This can result in policies that favor corporate profits over the well-being of society as a whole.

Additionally, corporate lobbies can create a barrier to entry for smaller businesses or organizations that do not have the same resources to influence policy. This can lead to a concentration of power and influence in the hands of a few large corporations, limiting competition and innovation in the marketplace.

Furthermore, the influence of corporate lobbies can lead to regulatory capture, where regulatory agencies are influenced by the industries they are meant to oversee. This can result in weak enforcement of regulations and inadequate protection for consumers and the environment.

Overall, the impact of corporate lobbies on policy formation can have far-reaching consequences for society, influencing the direction of policy in ways that may not always serve the public interest. It is important for policymakers and the public to be aware of the influence of corporate lobbies and work to ensure that policy decisions are made in the best interest of society as a whole.

The influence of corporate lobbies on policy formation is a topic of great concern and debate. As democracy and political enthusiasts, it is essential for us to understand the intricate relationship between corporate interests and democratic decision-making. In this subchapter, we will delve into the various aspects of this complex issue and shed light on its implications for the fate of democracy.

One of the fundamental questions we must address is the role of money in politics and its impact on democratic processes. Corporate lobbies, backed by substantial financial resources, have the ability to shape political agendas and sway policy outcomes in their favor. This raises concerns about the fairness and integrity of our democratic system, as the interests of wealthy corporations may supersede the needs and aspirations of ordinary citizens.

Understanding the power of interest groups in shaping political agendas is crucial in comprehending the impact of corporate lobbies on policy formation. These groups, representing various industries and sectors, employ sophisticated lobbying techniques to advance their interests. Through campaign contributions, direct lobbying, and the cultivation of relationships with politicians, they exert significant influence on the decision-making process. We will delve into the strategies employed by corporate lobbies and their implications for democratic outcomes.

The impact of corporate lobbies on policy formation is an incredibly intricate and multi-dimensional matter. It ignites important inquiries regarding the overwhelming power of finances in politics, the surge of populism, the significance of interest groups, and the profound influence of media on democratic outcomes. As ardent champions of democracy and political enthusiasts, it is absolutely imperative for us to meticulously scrutinize these dynamics and ardently strive for an equitable and all-encompassing democratic system that genuinely reflects the true will of the people.

The Role of Money in Politics and its Impact on Democratic Processes. The risk of corruption

Money plays a significant role in politics, as it is often used to fund political campaigns, advertise, and promote a candidate's platform. While money is necessary for candidates to effectively campaign and communicate with voters, the influence of money in politics can also have negative impacts on democratic processes.

One of the main concerns with the role of money in politics is the risk of corruption. When wealthy individuals, corporations, or special interest groups donate large sums of money to political campaigns, there is a risk that they may seek to influence politicians in exchange for their financial support. This can lead to politicians prioritizing the interests of their wealthy donors over the needs and concerns of the general public, undermining the democratic process.

The influence of money in politics can also lead to unequal representation, as candidates who are able to raise large amounts of money may have an advantage over those who cannot. This can result in a lack of diversity among elected officials, as candidates from marginalized communities or with limited financial resources may struggle to compete in elections.

Additionally, the reliance on money in politics can create barriers for new and independent candidates to enter the political arena. Candidates who do not have access to large donor networks or personal wealth may struggle to fund their campaigns, making it difficult for them to compete with established politicians who have significant financial backing.

Overall, the role of money in politics can have a significant impact on democratic processes, potentially leading to corruption, unequal representation, and barriers for new and independent candidates. It is important for regulations to be in place to limit the influence of money in politics and ensure that political campaigns are transparent and accountable to the public.

Undeniably, money has wielded an immense influence in politics for ages, leaving no room to disregard its impact on democratic processes. In the present age, the escalating power of money in politics has ignited fervent debates questioning the very essence of democracy and the detrimental effects of financial lobbies and corporate interests on decision-making.

One of the key issues surrounding money in politics is the question of whether it truly represents the interests of the people or if it merely serves the agendas of those who can afford to finance political campaigns. This debate lies at the heart of the real democracy, where the tension between political financial lobbies and populism often arises. While financial lobbies may bring economic expertise and resources to the table, their influence raises concerns about the potential distortion of democratic decision-making.

Compilation of unethical behaviors in political campaigns and presidential elections worldwide

1. Watergate scandal (United States, 1972) - The Watergate scandal involved illegal activities undertaken by members of the Nixon administration to secure the re-election of President Richard Nixon. This included the break-in at the Democratic National Committee headquarters and subsequent cover-up.
2. Iran-Contra affair (United States, 1980s) - The Iran-Contra affair involved senior officials in the Reagan administration secretly selling weapons to Iran in exchange for the release of American hostages and using the proceeds to fund Contra rebels in Nicaragua, despite a congressional ban on such support.
3. Cash-for-votes scandal (India, 2008) - A scandal in which members of the Indian parliament were caught on camera accepting bribes in exchange for their votes in a crucial confidence motion.
4. Cambridge Analytica scandal (United States, 2016) - Cambridge Analytica, a political consulting firm, was found to have improperly accessed the personal data of millions of Facebook users to target and influence voters during the 2016 US presidential election.
5. Jammeh's reelection (The Gambia, 2016) - Former Gambian President Yahya Jammeh was accused of rigging the 2016 presidential election through voter intimidation, media censorship, and other forms of electoral fraud.
6. 1MDB scandal (Malaysia, 2015) - The 1MDB scandal involved the misappropriation of billions of dollars from a Malaysian government investment fund, with the funds allegedly used to finance the election campaign of former Prime Minister Najib Razak.
7. Petrobras scandal (Brazil, 2014) - The Petrobras scandal involved a massive corruption scheme at the state-owned oil company, with politicians from various parties accused of accepting bribes in exchange for contracts and political support.

8. Russian interference in the 2016 US presidential election - The US intelligence community concluded that Russia interfered in the 2016 presidential election through a combination of social media manipulation, hacking, and other tactics to undermine American democracy and help Donald Trump win the presidency.

Exploring the Influence of Money in Political e presidential Campaigns

Money plays a significant role in political campaigns, especially in presidential campaigns. Candidates need funds to run their campaigns effectively, from paying staff and running ads to organizing events and traveling across the country. The influence of money in political campaigns can be seen in various aspects:

1. Fundraising: Presidential campaigns require large amounts of money to be successful, and candidates spend a significant amount of time fundraising. They rely on donations from individuals, corporations, and political action committees to finance their campaigns. The more money a candidate raises, the more resources they have to reach out to voters and promote their message.
2. Advertising: Money is essential for advertising in political campaigns, particularly in presidential races where candidates need to reach a national audience. Television ads, digital ads, and mailers are all costly, and candidates with more money can afford to run more ads and reach more voters.
3. Staff and Infrastructure: Campaigns need to hire staff, rent office space, and invest in technology and infrastructure to run smoothly. Having more money allows candidates to hire more experienced staff, set up more field offices, and use advanced data analytics to target voters effectively.

4. Travel and Events: Presidential candidates need to travel extensively to campaign across the country and attend events such as debates, town halls, and fundraisers. Travel expenses can add up quickly, and candidates with more money can afford to travel more frequently and reach out to voters in more states.
5. Influence: Money can also influence the outcome of elections by giving certain candidates an advantage. Wealthy donors and special interest groups can donate large sums of money to candidates, leading to concerns about the influence of money on political decisions and policies.

Overall, money plays a crucial role in presidential campaigns, shaping the candidates' ability to reach voters, promote their message, and ultimately win the election. While fundraising and spending money are necessary aspects of running a successful campaign, there are also concerns about the influence of money on the political process and the potential for wealthy donors to have undue influence on elections.

In the modern political landscape, the influence of money in political campaigns has become a subject of great concern for democracy lovers and political enthusiasts alike. This subchapter delves into the intricate relationship between money, media, and the fate of democracy, highlighting the various ways in which financial interests shape political outcomes.

By pouring substantial amounts of money into political campaigns, corporate lobbies gain unprecedented access and influence over elected officials, raising questions about the true representation of the people's interests.

When campaigns become increasingly expensive, candidates are forced to rely on wealthy donors and special interest groups to fund their campaigns. This creates a system where politicians are beholden to their financial backers, compromising the integrity of the democratic process and undermining the notion of equal representation.

In conclusion, the pervasive influence of monetary contributions in political campaigns represents a pivotal facet of democracy that warrants closer scrutiny. The formidable sway wielded by corporate lobbies, the intricate interplay between financial resources and political activities, the burgeoning tide of populism, the formidable impact of interest groups, and the profound imprint of media collectively converge to mold democratic outcomes. Comprehending and tackling these matters is indispensable for upholding the tenets of democracy and guaranteeing the authentic manifestation of the populace's interests.

How much cost a presidential campaign in USA? List of the 10 most expensive

The cost of a presidential campaign in the USA can vary greatly depending on the candidate, the political climate, and other factors. Here is a list of the 10 most expensive presidential campaigns in US history:

1. 2020 - Joe Biden (D) - $1.3 billion
2. 2016 - Hillary Clinton (D) - $1.2 billion

3. 2012 - Barack Obama (D) - $1.1 billion
4. 2008 - Barack Obama (D) - $1.1 billion
5. 2004 - George W. Bush (R) - $367 million
6. 2000 - Al Gore (D) - $335 million
7. 1996 - Bill Clinton (D) - $251 million
8. 2016 - Donald Trump (R) - $398 million
9. 2008 - John McCain (R) - $400 million
10. 2012 - Mitt Romney (R) - $433 million

These figures include money spent by the candidates' campaigns, as well as money spent by independent groups supporting or opposing the candidates.

The list of 20 most expensive election campaign in the world

1. 2020 United States Presidential Election - $14 billion
2. 2016 United States Presidential Election - $6.5 billion
3. 2012 United States Presidential Election - $6 billion
4. 2019 Indian General Election - $8.65 billion
5. 2017 French Presidential Election - $2.4 billion
6. 2019 European Parliament Election - $1.8 billion
7. 2019 Canadian Federal Election - $1.3 billion
8. 2019 Australian Federal Election - $1.2 billion
9. 2016 United Kingdom European Union Membership Referendum - $1.1 billion
10. 2019 Israeli Legislative Election - $1 billion
11. 2018 Mexican General Election - $800 million
12. 2018 Brazilian General Election - $700 million
13. 2018 United States Midterm Elections - $5.2 billion
14. 2018 Russian Presidential Election - $450 million
15. 2017 United Kingdom General Election - $400 million
16. 2017 German Federal Election - $350 million

17. 2016 Spanish General Election - $300 million
18. 2019 South African General Election - $280 million
19. 2018 Italian General Election - $250 million
20. 2018 Swedish General Election - $200 million

Understanding the Role of Political Donations in Shaping Policies

Political donations play a significant role in shaping policies and influencing decision-making in the political arena. Donations from individuals, corporations, and interest groups can provide financial support to political candidates and parties, allowing them to fund their campaigns, reach out to voters, and promote their policy agendas.

In return for these donations, politicians may feel obligated to support the interests of their donors and prioritize their policy preferences. This can lead to a situation where policies are influenced by the desires of wealthy donors or special interest groups, rather than reflecting the needs and priorities of the general public.

Political donations can also be used strategically by donors to gain access and influence over policymakers. By donating large sums of money to political candidates or parties, donors can gain favor with elected officials and potentially secure meetings, influence policy decisions, or receive favorable treatment.

Furthermore, the influence of political donations can extend beyond individual policies and shape the overall political landscape. Donors may support candidates who align with their interests, leading to the election of officials who are more likely to support policies that benefit those donors. This can create a cycle of influence where donors continue to support candidates who will advance their agendas, further consolidating their power and influence over the political process.

Overall, the role of political donations in shaping policies highlights the importance of transparency, accountability, and campaign finance reform in order to ensure that the interests of the public are prioritized over the influence of wealthy donors and special interest groups. By understanding the impact of political donations on policymaking, we can work towards a more equitable and democratic political system that represents the interests of all citizens.

So we can affirm that the role of political donations cannot be underestimated. These financial contributions have a significant impact on shaping policies and determining the direction of our democracies. This subchapter will delve into the intricate relationship between political donations, interest groups, media, and the fate of democracy.

Examining the Effects of Wealth Disparity on Democratic Representation

In recent years, the world has witnessed a growing wealth disparity among its citizens. This disparity has had a profound impact on democratic representation, shaping the political landscape and influencing key decision-making processes. In this subchapter, we delve into the effects of wealth disparity on democratic representation, exploring its consequences for the real democracy, the influence of corporate lobbies, the role of money in politics, the rise of populism, the power of interest groups, and the role of media.

Wealth disparity can have significant effects on democratic representation in a society. When there is a large gap between the wealthy and the rest of the population, it can lead to unequal political power and influence. Wealthy individuals and corporations often have more resources to contribute to political campaigns, lobby for their interests, and influence decision-making processes.

This can result in policies that primarily benefit the wealthy, rather than the broader population. For example, tax policies may favor the wealthy by providing tax breaks or loopholes that allow them to pay lower tax rates than the average citizen. This can lead to a decrease in funding for important social programs and services that benefit the majority of the population.

Furthermore, wealthier individuals may have more access to politicians and decision-makers, leading to a situation where their interests are prioritized over those of the general public. This can undermine the principles of democracy, where all citizens are supposed to have an equal voice in the political process.

In addition, wealth inequality can also impact who is able to run for political office. Running for office requires a significant amount of financial resources, from campaign expenses to personal finances needed to support oneself during the campaign. This can deter individuals from lower-income backgrounds from seeking political office, leading to a lack of diverse representation in government.

Overall, wealth disparity can have a detrimental impact on democratic representation by skewing political power and influence towards the wealthy, limiting the representation of marginalized communities, and perpetuating policies that benefit the wealthy at the expense of the broader population. Addressing wealth inequality is essential for ensuring a more equitable and inclusive democratic system.

The real democracy, as we envision it, should be a system that ensures equal representation and participation for all citizens. However, wealth disparity has skewed this ideal, favoring the interests of the rich and powerful. The influence of corporate lobbies on democratic decision-making has become increasingly prevalent, as deep-pocketed interest groups manipulate the political agenda to serve their own self-interest. This influence often comes at the expense of the average citizen, whose voice is drowned out by the powerful few. It is crucial that we strive to address this imbalance and work towards a more inclusive and fair democratic system that truly represents the diverse voices of our society.

Wealth disparity profoundly impacts democratic representation, causing severe damage to the core principles of equal representation and participation. It shamelessly favors the interests of the affluent and influential, leaving the voices of ordinary citizens unheard. The pervasive influence of corporate lobbies, the corrupting role of money in politics, the alarming rise of populism, the undue power of interest groups, and the manipulative role of media, all perpetuate this intricate web of injustice. To secure the future of democracy, it is absolutely imperative that we confront these pressing issues head-on and relentlessly strive towards a system that genuinely upholds and represents the diverse interests of every single citizen.

Chapter 2: The Rise of Populism and its Effects on Democracy

Understanding Populism and its Ideologies in respect of traditional parties as democratic and Republican

Populism is a political ideology that focuses on the concerns and interests of ordinary people, often pitting them against a perceived elite or establishment. Populist movements typically advocate for policies that address the needs of the working class and emphasize nationalism, protectionism, and anti-globalization.

In the context of traditional parties like the Democratic and Republican parties in the United States, populism has manifested in different ways. On the Democratic side, there has been a rise of progressive populism, championed by figures like Bernie Sanders and Elizabeth Warren. These politicians have focused on issues like income inequality, healthcare reform, and workers' rights, appealing to the frustrations of many working-class Americans who feel left behind by the political establishment.

On the Republican side, populism has taken the form of right-wing populism, exemplified by figures like Donald Trump. Trump's brand of populism has emphasized nationalism, anti-immigration policies, and a rejection of traditional political norms. His rhetoric has resonated with many Americans who feel disillusioned with the political establishment and who are looking for a strong leader to shake up the status quo.

Both Democratic and Republican parties have had to grapple with the rise of populism within their ranks, as it challenges the traditional party structures and ideologies. Populism has forced these parties to adapt to the changing political landscape and address the concerns of their constituents in new ways. However, the extent to which these parties embrace populism and its ideologies varies, with some factions within each party resisting populist movements and advocating for more traditional policies and approaches.

So populism has emerged as a powerful force in contemporary politics, challenging traditional democratic systems and reshaping the political landscape. In this subchapter, we will delve into the intricacies of populism, exploring its ideologies and the implications it has for democracy.

However, others express concerns about the rise of populism and its effects on democracy. They argue that populism can be manipulative and divisive, relying on simplistic narratives and scapegoating to gain support. Populist leaders often undermine democratic institutions and norms, eroding the checks and balances that are crucial for a healthy democracy.

Understanding populism and its ideologies is essential for anyone interested in the fate of democracy. Populism has both its proponents and detractors, and its impact on democratic systems is complex and multifaceted. By exploring the influence of corporate lobbies, the role of money in politics, and the power of interest groups in shaping political agendas, we can gain a deeper understanding of the rise of populism and its effects on democracy.

Additionally, analyzing the role of media and its influence on democratic outcomes is crucial for comprehending the dynamics of contemporary politics. It is important to recognize that populism can take on different forms in various countries and regions, influenced by historical, social, and economic factors. Moreover, the relationship between populism and authoritarianism should be examined, as some populist leaders have displayed authoritarian tendencies that can threaten democratic principles. In order to address the challenges posed by populism, it is necessary to promote transparency, accountability, and civic engagement in political processes. Furthermore, fostering inclusive and participatory democracies can help counter the divisive and exclusionary rhetoric often associated with populist movements.

Ultimately, a nuanced understanding of populism and its implications for democracy is crucial for safeguarding democratic values and institutions in an increasingly polarized world.

Political theory of Populism in the democratic system

Populism is a political ideology that pits the common people against a perceived elite or establishment, often championing the interests and concerns of ordinary citizens. In a democratic system, populism can manifest in various forms and have both positive and negative implications.

One of the key tenets of populism in a democratic system is the idea of direct representation of the people, bypassing traditional political institutions and elites. Populist leaders often claim to speak for the silent majority and promise to address their grievances and concerns. This can lead to a more participatory form of democracy, with increased engagement and mobilization of citizens.

However, populism can also be detrimental to democracy, as it tends to polarize society and undermine the rule of law. Populist leaders may use inflammatory rhetoric and appeal to emotions rather than reason, leading to a breakdown of civil discourse and the erosion of democratic norms and institutions. Populism can also be associated with authoritarian tendencies, as leaders may seek to consolidate power and weaken checks and balances.

In terms of policy, populist movements often focus on issues such as economic inequality, immigration, and national identity. They may advocate for protectionist measures, such as trade tariffs and immigration restrictions, in order to protect the interests of the domestic population. Populism can also be associated with a rejection of international institutions and agreements, as well as a distrust of experts and mainstream media. Additionally, populist movements tend to prioritize the concerns of the working class and rural populations, often portraying themselves as champions of the ordinary citizen against the elite establishment. They may also promote nationalist sentiments and emphasize the importance of preserving cultural traditions and values. Overall, populism thrives on tapping into the grievances and fears of the populace, offering simple solutions to complex problems and promising to bring about change that benefits the common people.

Overall, populism in a democratic system can be a double-edged sword. While it can give voice to marginalized groups and challenge the status quo, it also poses a threat to democratic values and institutions. Populist movements have the potential to bring about much-needed change and shake up the established power dynamics, but they must be carefully monitored to prevent any erosion of democratic principles. It is crucial for citizens and political leaders to engage in critical analysis of populist rhetoric and actions, ensuring that they do not infringe upon the rights of individuals or undermine the foundations of democracy. By maintaining a vigilant approach and holding populist movements accountable, we can safeguard the integrity of our democratic system and protect the rights and freedoms of all citizens.

Defining Populism and its Historical Roots

Populism is a complex and multifaceted political ideology that has gained significant traction in recent years, challenging the traditional structures of democracy. In order to understand its impact on our political landscape, it is essential to delve into its historical roots and examine how it has evolved over time.

At its core, populism can be defined as a political approach that seeks to appeal to the interests and concerns of ordinary people, often positioning itself as a champion of the common man against the elites. However, the term populism is often used in different contexts and can encompass a wide range of ideologies and movements.

The historical roots of populism can be traced back to the late 19th century agrarian movements in the United States, such as the

People's Party, which emerged in response to the economic hardships faced by farmers. These movements aimed to challenge the dominance of the wealthy elites and advocate for the rights and interests of the working class.

In Europe, populism took a different form, emerging as a response to the rise of industrialization and the social and economic changes that accompanied it. Figures like Benito Mussolini in Italy and Adolf Hitler in Germany exploited the grievances of the working class and employed populist rhetoric to gain support for their authoritarian regimes.

Today, populism has taken on new dimensions, fueled by a combination of economic uncertainty, growing inequality, and a perceived disenchantment with traditional political establishments. The rise of populist leaders and movements across the globe, from Donald Trump in the United States to Jair Bolsonaro in Brazil, has reshaped the political landscape and raised important questions about the future of democracy.

One of the key challenges posed by populism is its potential to undermine democratic institutions and processes. Populist leaders often employ divisive rhetoric, appealing to emotions and exploiting fears to gain support. This can lead to a polarized political climate and hinder constructive dialogue and compromise.

Furthermore, the influence of corporate lobbies and their financial power has also played a significant role in shaping the populist narrative. The close relationship between big business and politics has led to concerns about the integrity of democratic decision-making, as corporate interests often take precedence over the needs and concerns of ordinary citizens.

The rise of populism has been accompanied by the proliferation of alternative media platforms that disseminate misinformation and propaganda. This has further deepened divisions within society and eroded trust in traditional media sources.

By delving into the historical roots and gradual development of populism, we can gain a deeper understanding of the obstacles it presents to the foundations of democratic governance, and delve into innovative approaches to ensuring the preservation of our political structures. Through a thorough examination of the impact of populism, corporate interests, financial influences in political decision-making, special interest groups, and media manipulation, we are able to pave the way for a future where democratic principles not only survive but flourish, allowing for an authentic representation of the collective voice of the populace.

Analyzing the Different Types of Populist Movements

Populist movements have gained significant attention in recent years, challenging traditional political structures and reshaping the democratic landscape. In this subchapter, we will delve into the various types of populist movements, their characteristics, and the impact they have on the fate of democracy.

One type of populist movement that has emerged is the anti-establishment movement. These movements arise from a deep dissatisfaction with the ruling elites and the perceived corruption and lack of representation in traditional political institutions. They often rally around charismatic leaders who promise to bring power back to the people and challenge the dominance of political and financial lobbies. The real democracy is at stake, and these movements seek to restore it by dismantling the influence of corporate lobbies on democratic decision-making.

Another type of populist movement focuses on the role of money in politics and its impact on democratic processes. These movements highlight the undue influence of wealthy individuals and corporations in shaping political agendas and decision-making. They argue that democracy should be based on the will of the people rather than the interests of a privileged few. As such, they advocate for campaign finance reform, stricter regulations on lobbying, and transparency in political financing.

Remember analyzing the different types of populist movements provides valuable insights into the challenges and opportunities they pose to democracy. By examining their characteristics, we can better understand how they impact the real democracy, the influence of corporate lobbies on democratic decision-making, the role of money in politics, the power of interest groups, and the role of media in shaping democratic outcomes. This knowledge is crucial for anyone interested in the fate of democracy and the future of political systems.

History of populism and the most prominent person who create this new way to interact in politics

Populism has a long history dating back to the late 19th century in the United States. It emerged as a political movement that aimed to represent the interests of the common people against the elite and established power structures. Populism often involves appeals to the emotions and concerns of ordinary citizens, and is characterized by a distrust of political elites and a desire for radical change.

One of the most prominent figures in the history of populism is William Jennings Bryan, a politician and orator who ran for president three times as the Democratic Party nominee in the late 19th and early 20th centuries. Bryan was a champion of the populist cause, advocating for the interests of farmers and working-class Americans against the wealthy industrialists and bankers of the time.

Bryan's most famous speech, the "Cross of Gold" speech delivered at the 1896 Democratic National Convention, called for the free coinage of silver as a way to combat the economic hardships facing farmers and workers. Although Bryan ultimately lost the election, his populist message and appeal to the common people helped to shape the political landscape of the time.

In more recent times, populist movements have emerged in countries around the world, with leaders such as Hugo Chávez in Venezuela, Recep Tayyip Erdoğan in Turkey, and Donald Trump in the United States adopting populist rhetoric and policies. These leaders have tapped into the grievances and frustrations of ordinary citizens, promising to address their concerns and challenge the existing political establishment.

Overall, populism continues to be a powerful force in politics, shaping the way leaders interact with the public and influencing the direction of policy and governance in many countries.

Examining the Populist Leaders and their Strategies

In recent years, the rise of populism has captured the attention of democracy and political enthusiasts worldwide. Populist leaders have emerged as influential figures, offering alternative approaches to governance and challenging the traditional political establishment. This subchapter delves into the phenomenon of populism, scrutinizing the strategies employed by populist leaders and their impact on democratic processes.

Populist leaders, often charismatic and adept at mobilizing support, have gained popularity by appealing to the frustrations and grievances of the people. They tap into the growing disillusionment with the political and economic elites, promising to champion the interests of the common citizens. By presenting themselves as outsiders, they create a sense of connection and empathy with the people, positioning themselves as the voice of the marginalized.

One of the key strategies employed by populist leaders is the utilization of media platforms to disseminate their messages and ideologies. They harness the power of social media, employing catchy slogans and simplistic narratives to capture the attention of the masses. By bypassing the traditional gatekeepers of information, populist leaders can directly communicate with their supporters, circumventing the influence of corporate lobbies and traditional media outlets.

1. Donald Trump - Former President of the United States and leader of the Republican Party. Known for his anti-establishment rhetoric and nationalist policies.
2. Jair Bolsonaro - President of Brazil and leader of the Social Liberal Party. Bolsonaro is known for his controversial statements and populist approach to governing.
3. Matteo Salvini - Former Deputy Prime Minister of Italy and leader of the right-wing League party. Salvini is known for his hardline stance on immigration and Eurosceptic views.
4. Viktor Orban - Prime Minister of Hungary and leader of the Fidesz party. Orban is known for his authoritarian policies and anti-immigrant stance.
5. Narendra Modi - Prime Minister of India and leader of the Bharatiya Janata Party. Modi is known for his Hindu nationalist agenda and populist appeal.
6. Recep Tayyip Erdogan - President of Turkey and leader of the Justice and Development Party. Erdogan is known for his authoritarian tendencies and populist rhetoric.
7. Rodrigo Duterte - President of the Philippines and leader of the PDP-Laban party. Duterte is known for his controversial war on drugs and anti-establishment stance.
8. Andrzej Duda - President of Poland and member of the Law and Justice party. Duda is known for his conservative policies and nationalist rhetoric.
9. Boris Johnson - Prime Minister of the United Kingdom and leader of the Conservative Party. Johnson is known for his populist approach to Brexit and nationalist policies.

10. Marine Le Pen - Leader of the National Rally party in France. Le Pen is known for her anti-immigrant stance and Eurosceptic views.
11. Khaled Ali - Egyptian politician and leader of the Bread and Freedom Party. Ali is known for his populist and socialist policies.
12. Evo Morales - Former President of Bolivia and leader of the Movement for Socialism party. Morales is known for his socialist policies and populist approach to governance.
13. Nicolás Maduro - President of Venezuela and leader of the United Socialist Party. Maduro is known for his authoritarian rule and populist rhetoric.
14. Bernie Sanders - American politician and leader of the Democratic Party. Sanders is known for his progressive policies and populist appeal.
1. Pablo Iglesias - Spanish politician and leader of the Podemos party. Iglesias is known for his anti-establishment stance and populist rhetoric.
2. Giuseppe Conte - Former Prime Minister of Italy and leader of the Five Star Movement. Conte is known for his anti-establishment policies and populist approach to governance.
3. Pedro Castillo - President of Peru and leader of the Free Peru party. Castillo is known for his socialist policies and anti-establishment stance.
4. Yair Lapid - Israeli politician and leader of the Yesh Atid party. Lapid is known for his centrist policies and populist appeal.
5. Alexis Tsipras - Former Prime Minister of Greece and leader of the Syriza party. Tsipras is known for his anti-austerity policies and populist rhetoric.
6. Annalena Baerbock - German politician and leader of the Green Party. Baerbock is known for her environmental policies and populist approach to politics.

Populism around the world: which counties they have populist movements

Populist movements have emerged in various countries around the world, including:

1. United States - The election of Donald Trump as President in 2016 is often seen as a result of populist sentiment in the country.
2. Brazil - Jair Bolsonaro, who was elected as President in 2018, is known for his populist and nationalist rhetoric.
3. Italy - The political party Five Star Movement, led by Luigi Di Maio and founded by comedian Beppe Grillo, has gained popularity in recent years.
4. Hungary - Prime Minister Viktor Orban and his Fidesz party have been criticized for their nationalist and anti-immigrant policies.
5. Philippines - President Rodrigo Duterte has been described as a populist leader for his tough stance on crime and drugs.
6. India - Prime Minister Narendra Modi and his Bharatiya Janata Party (BJP) have been accused of promoting a populist agenda.
7. Turkey - President Recep Tayyip Erdogan has been criticized for his authoritarian tendencies and populist rhetoric.
8. Poland - The Law and Justice party, led by Jaroslaw Kaczynski, has been accused of promoting populist and nationalist policies.

These are just a few examples of countries where populist movements have gained traction in recent years.

Investigating the Tactics Employed by Populist Leaders

Populism has emerged as a powerful force in modern politics, challenging traditional democratic processes and institutions. In this subchapter, we will delve into the tactics employed by populist leaders and their impact on the fate of democracy.

Populist leaders often tap into the frustrations and grievances of the people, presenting themselves as the sole voice of the marginalized and disenchanted. They employ a range of strategies to gain support, such as simplifying complex issues, using emotional language, and offering quick and easy solutions to deep-rooted problems. By framing themselves as the champions of the people against a corrupt and out-of-touch elite, they create a sense of us-versus-them, dividing society along populist lines.

One of the key tactics employed by populist leaders is the use of rhetoric that stokes fear and resentment. By scapegoating certain groups, such as immigrants or ethnic minorities, they redirect anger and frustration away from structural issues and towards vulnerable populations. This not only fuels division within society but also undermines the principles of inclusivity and equality that are fundamental to democracy.

Furthermore, populist leaders often rely on the power of the media to amplify their messages and reach a wider audience. They understand the influence of media in shaping public opinion and use it to their advantage. By utilizing social media platforms and employing catchy slogans, they are able to bypass traditional gatekeepers and directly connect with their supporters. However, this reliance on media can also lead to the spread of misinformation and the erosion of trust in reliable sources of information.

Another tactic employed by populist leaders is their rejection of established political norms and institutions. They position themselves as outsiders who will upend the existing order and bring about radical change. While this may appeal to those who feel disillusioned with the status quo, it also poses a threat to the stability and functioning of democratic processes. By undermining the checks and balances that are essential to democracy, populist leaders risk consolidating their own power and diminishing the voices of dissent.

Understanding the tactics employed by populist leaders is crucial in assessing their impact on the fate of democracy. By exploiting public grievances, utilizing media channels, and challenging established norms, they can reshape the political landscape. However, it is important to critically examine the consequences of these tactics, as they can undermine democratic principles and lead to the erosion of democratic processes. By remaining vigilant and informed, democracy and political lovers can play a crucial role in safeguarding the future of democracy.

Analyzing the Appeal of Populist Rhetoric to the Masses

Populist rhetoric tends to resonate with the masses for a variety of reasons. One key aspect is its simplicity and directness. Populist leaders often use straightforward language and present issues in a way that is easy for the average person to understand. This can be appealing to individuals who may feel disconnected from the political process or overwhelmed by complex policy discussions.

Additionally, populist rhetoric often taps into common grievances or frustrations that many people may have. Populist leaders often frame themselves as champions of the "ordinary" people and position themselves as fighting against elites or entrenched interests. This can be particularly appealing to individuals who feel marginalized or left behind by the current political system.

Furthermore, populist rhetoric often relies on emotional appeals and can be highly effective at tapping into people's fears, anxieties, and desires for change. By framing issues in terms of "us vs. them" or painting a dire picture of the current state of affairs, populist leaders can create a sense of urgency and mobilize support among the masses.

Overall, the appeal of populist rhetoric to the masses lies in its ability to simplify complex issues, resonate with common grievances, and tap into people's emotions. By presenting themselves as champions of the people and offering simple solutions to complex problems, populist leaders can garner widespread support and mobilize a broad base of followers.

In recent years, the rise of populism has captured the attention of both political pundits and ordinary citizens. Populist leaders, with their captivating rhetoric and promises of change, have managed to galvanize large segments of the population. But why is it that populist rhetoric seems to resonate so strongly with the masses? In this subchapter, we will delve into the various factors that contribute to the appeal of populist rhetoric to the masses.

One of the key reasons behind the appeal of populist rhetoric is its ability to tap into the frustration and disillusionment felt by many members of society. The real democracy, as we know it, has often been criticized for its perceived shortcomings, including the influence of political financial lobbies. Populist leaders are adept at identifying these grievances and presenting themselves as champions of the people against the establishment. By positioning themselves as outsiders, they are able to establish a connection with the masses who feel marginalized by the current political system.

Populist leaders frequently bring attention to this matter and pledge to combat the excessive power of corporate interests. This strikes a chord with people who believe that their opinions are being ignored by influential groups. Populist leaders commonly support reforming campaign finance, vowing to diminish the impact of money in politics. This commitment to creating a fairer political landscape resonates with individuals who believe that their votes are being marginalized by wealthy donors.

Populist leaders are highly adept at identifying and capitalizing on the simmering discontent and dissatisfaction experienced by various factions within society, effectively steering it towards advancing their own political objectives. Through pledging to tackle the unique grievances of these groups, they succeed in uniting a diverse array of advocates. Furthermore, these leaders exhibit a remarkable proficiency in leveraging various media platforms to magnify their messaging and engage a broader audience. By circumventing conventional communication channels, they are able to directly connect with their backers and cultivate a devoted base of supporters.

The appeal of populist rhetoric to the masses can be attributed to a combination of factors. Firstly, the frustration with the existing political system, which often fails to address the needs and concerns of the general population, pushes individuals towards leaders who promise change and reform. Secondly, the influence of corporate lobbies and big money in politics cannot be overlooked, as these entities often have undue influence on decision-making processes. Additionally, the rise of interest groups and their ability to mobilize support for populist movements further contributes to the appeal of such leaders. Lastly, the power of media in shaping public opinion and promoting certain narratives plays a crucial role in amplifying populist rhetoric. As advocates for democracy and political enthusiasts, it is imperative for us to delve into these dynamics and critically assess the impact of populism on our democratic processes.

Assessing the Impact of Populism on Democratic Institutions

Populism, as a political ideology that pits "the people" against an elite or establishment, has gained traction in recent years and has had a significant impact on democratic institutions around the world. While populism can sometimes serve as a check on entrenched power and give voice to marginalized groups, it also poses a threat to democratic norms and institutions in several ways.

One of the key impacts of populism on democratic institutions is the erosion of trust in political institutions and processes. Populist leaders often portray themselves as the sole voice of the people, undermining the legitimacy of other branches of government, political parties, and the media. This can lead to a breakdown in the checks and balances that are essential for a functioning democracy, as well as a weakening of the rule of law.

Populism can also lead to the polarization of society, as populist leaders tend to frame political issues in terms of "us versus them." This can exacerbate divisions within society, making it harder to find common ground and reach consensus on important issues. In extreme cases, populism can even lead to the erosion of civil liberties and the targeting of minority groups as scapegoats for societal problems.

Furthermore, populism can undermine the independence of key democratic institutions, such as the judiciary and the media. Populist leaders often seek to undermine the credibility of these institutions in order to consolidate their own power and silence dissent. This can have serious implications for the rule of law and freedom of expression, which are essential components of a healthy democracy.

Overall, while populism can sometimes serve as a wake-up call for established political elites and lead to much-needed reforms, it also poses a significant threat to democratic institutions. In order to safeguard democracy in the face of populism, it is essential to strengthen institutions that uphold the rule of law, protect civil liberties, and promote transparency and accountability in government. This may require a concerted effort by civil society, political leaders, and ordinary citizens to push back against populist tendencies and defend the principles of democracy.

Populism has emerged as a powerful force in contemporary politics, challenging the traditional democratic institutions that have long been the bedrock of our societies. In this subchapter, we will delve into the complex and multifaceted relationship between populism and democratic institutions, exploring the various ways in which this phenomenon has shaped the fate of democracy.

One of the central debates surrounding populism is its impact on democratic decision-making. Critics argue that populism tends to undermine the democratic process by appealing to emotions and simplistic solutions, rather than engaging in rational and evidence-based discourse. This raises concerns about the quality and integrity of democratic decision-making. We will examine the extent to which populism has influenced the policy-making process and whether it has provided a genuine alternative to the influence of corporate lobbies.

Is populism beneficial or harmful to democracy?

It depends on the context and the actions of the populist leader or movement. Populism can be both good and bad for democracy. On one hand, populism can mobilize and engage citizens who feel disenfranchised or marginalized, leading to increased political participation and accountability.

Populist movements can also bring attention to important issues that may have been ignored by mainstream political parties. However, on the other hand, populism can also be detrimental to democracy if it undermines democratic institutions, promotes divisive rhetoric, and erodes the rule of law. Populist leaders may also exploit fear and anger to consolidate power and suppress dissent, which can have long-lasting negative effects on the democratic system.

Ultimately, the impact of populism on democracy depends on how it is wielded and whether it upholds democratic values and principles, highlighting the importance of critically examining the actions and motivations of populist movements in order to safeguard the integrity of democratic processes.

Exploring the Erosion of Democratic Norms in Populist Regimes or populist governments

Populist regimes have been on the rise in recent years, with leaders like Donald Trump in the United States, Jair Bolsonaro in Brazil, and Viktor Orban in Hungary gaining power by appealing to the grievances of the people against the political establishment. While populism can be a useful tool for challenging the status quo and giving a voice to marginalized groups, it also poses a significant threat to democratic norms and institutions.

One of the key ways in which populist regimes erode democratic norms is through their attacks on the media and freedom of speech. Populist leaders often demonize journalists and news outlets that criticize them, labeling them as "fake news" or "enemies of the people." This not only undermines the credibility of the press but also creates a climate of fear and self-censorship, as journalists face harassment, intimidation, and even violence for reporting on government abuses.

Another common tactic used by populist regimes to erode democratic norms is the centralization of power in the hands of the leader. Populist leaders often seek to weaken the checks and balances that are essential for a functioning democracy, such as independent judiciary, legislative oversight, and a free and fair electoral process. They may also manipulate the legal system to target political opponents, suppress dissent, and consolidate their own power.

Furthermore, populist regimes often engage in divisive rhetoric and scapegoating of marginalized groups, such as immigrants, minorities, and political dissidents. This can further polarize society, fueling hatred and intolerance, and undermining the principles of equality and human rights that are fundamental to democracy.

In conclusion, the erosion of democratic norms in populist regimes poses a serious threat to the rule of law, human rights, and the principles of good governance. It is essential for civil society, international organizations, and democratic governments to remain vigilant and push back against the authoritarian tendencies of populist leaders, in order to protect and defend democracy for future generations.

The world has witnessed a surge in populist movements and the rise of leaders who challenge the established norms of democracy. These figures, often charismatic and appealing to the frustrations of the masses, have reshaped political landscapes and raised important questions about the erosion of democratic norms. In this subchapter, we delve into the complex relationship between populism and democracy, shedding light on the consequences of this phenomenon for our political systems.

Populist leaders often present themselves as champions of the people, promising to bring power back to the masses. However, we critically assess the consequences of their rhetoric and policies for democratic institutions. We investigate how populist regimes can erode checks and balances, suppress dissenting voices, and concentrate power in the hands of a few. By examining case studies from around the world, we paint a comprehensive picture of the challenges posed by populism to the sustainability of democratic systems.

Evaluating the Threat of Authoritarianism in Populist Governments

Authoritarianism in populist governments poses a significant threat to democracy, freedom, and human rights. Populist leaders often exploit public fears and insecurities to consolidate power and undermine democratic institutions. They scapegoat marginalized groups, attack the media, and centralize power in order to silence dissent and control the narrative.

Authoritarian populism erodes the checks and balances that are essential for a functioning democracy, leading to a concentration of power in the hands of a few individuals. This can result in the erosion of civil liberties, the suppression of political opposition, and the weakening of independent institutions such as the judiciary, media, and civil society organizations.

Additionally, authoritarian populist governments often promote a divisive and exclusionary form of nationalism, which can lead to the marginalization and persecution of minority groups. This can have serious consequences for social cohesion and the protection of human rights.

To evaluate the threat of authoritarianism in populist governments, it is important to closely monitor their actions and policies. This includes assessing their respect for the rule of law, their commitment to democratic principles, and their treatment of political opponents and marginalized groups. It is also essential to scrutinize their rhetoric and propaganda, as well as their attempts to undermine independent institutions and consolidate power.

Ultimately, it is crucial for civil society organizations, the media, and international actors to remain vigilant and hold authoritarian populist governments accountable for their actions. By upholding democratic values and advocating for human rights, we can help prevent the erosion of democracy and the rise of authoritarianism in populist governments.

In recent years, the rise of populism has shaken the foundations of democracies around the world. While populism can provide a platform for marginalized voices and foster a sense of political participation, it also carries the inherent risk of authoritarianism.

Populist movements often emerge as a response to a perceived loss of control over political and economic systems. They capitalize on the frustrations and grievances of the people, promising to restore power to the masses. However, the very nature of populism, with its emphasis on a strong charismatic leader and the direct connection between the leader and the people, can pave the way for authoritarian tendencies to take hold.

One of the key elements in assessing the threat of authoritarianism in populist governments is the influence of corporate lobbies on democratic decision-making. As populists come to power, they may prioritize the interests of certain groups, including corporate entities, over the broader democratic principles. This can lead to the erosion of checks and balances, as well as the concentration of power in the hands of a few.

Populist leaders, often charismatic and persuasive, can be susceptible to external influences, including financial support from interest groups or wealthy individuals. This can undermine the integrity of the democratic system, as policies and decisions may be swayed by those with deep pockets rather than the will of the people.

Furthermore, the power of interest groups in shaping political agendas becomes particularly significant in the context of populist governments. As these movements gain traction, interest groups may seek to exploit the populist rhetoric and push their own self-serving agendas. This can further marginalize certain segments of society and limit the inclusivity of the democratic process.

Populist leaders often rely on the manipulation of information and the creation of alternative narratives to maintain their popularity. This can include the demonization of opposition, the spread of misinformation, and the erosion of trust in traditional media sources. Such tactics can contribute to the consolidation of power and the erosion of democratic norms.

While populism can be a force for positive change in democracies, it also carries the potential for authoritarianism. The influence of corporate lobbies, the role of money in politics, the power of interest groups, and the manipulation of media are all factors that contribute to this threat. As democracy and political enthusiasts, it is crucial for us to remain vigilant and actively engage in the protection of democratic values to ensure that the revolution will truly be televised. It is essential for us to educate ourselves on the complexities of political systems, advocate for transparency and accountability in government, and promote inclusivity and diversity in decision-making processes. By actively participating in civic engagement, holding our leaders accountable, and standing up against corruption and injustice, we can work towards a more just and equitable society for all.

Chapter 3: The Power of Interest Groups in Shaping Political Agendas

Understanding Interest Groups and their Objectives

Interest groups, also known as pressure groups or lobbying groups, are organizations formed by individuals who share a common interest or goal and seek to influence public policy decisions. These groups work to advocate for their members' interests and shape public opinion on specific issues. Interest groups can vary widely in terms of their size, scope, and goals, but they all share the common objective of influencing government decision-making.

The primary objectives of interest groups can include:

1. Advocating for specific policies or legislation: Interest groups work to promote policies and laws that align with their members' interests. They may engage in lobbying efforts, public campaigns, and grassroots organizing to push for legislative change.
2. Influencing public opinion: Interest groups seek to shape public opinion on specific issues by raising awareness, providing information, and promoting their perspective through media campaigns and other communication channels.
3. Building coalitions: Interest groups often collaborate with other organizations, businesses, and individuals who share similar goals in order to amplify their collective voice and increase their influence.
4. Providing a platform for advocacy: Interest groups serve as a platform for individuals to come together and advocate for their shared

interests. They provide a forum for members to engage in collective action and work towards achieving their goals.
5. Monitoring government actions: Interest groups closely monitor government decisions and policies that may impact their members. They work to hold elected officials accountable and ensure that their interests are represented in the decision-making process.

Overall, interest groups play a crucial role in the political process by representing the interests of specific segments of society and advocating for policy changes that benefit their members. By mobilizing resources, building coalitions, and engaging in advocacy efforts, interest groups work to shape public policy and influence government decision-making.

Interest groups play a significant role in shaping democratic processes and outcomes. These groups represent specific sectors or ideologies and aim to influence political decision-making. In this subchapter, we will explore the objectives of interest groups and their impact on democracy, with a particular focus on the influence of corporate lobbies, the role of money in politics, the rise of populism, and the power of media.

The power of interest groups in shaping political agendas cannot be underestimated. These groups have the resources, expertise, and networks to effectively advocate for their interests. Through lobbying, public campaigns, and media influence, interest groups can shape public opinion and exert pressure on policymakers to adopt their preferred policies. This dynamic raises questions about the extent to which democratic decision-making truly reflects the will of the people.

The role of the Lobbies in Democracy

Lobbies play a significant role in a democracy by representing the interests of various groups and advocating for their positions to policymakers. They serve as a link between citizens and government, providing valuable information and expertise on specific issues.

Lobbies also help to ensure that a diverse range of voices and perspectives are heard in the decision-making process, contributing to a more inclusive and representative democracy. By organizing and mobilizing support for their causes, lobbies can influence policy outcomes and hold elected officials accountable.

However, there are growing concerns among the public and policymakers alike regarding the outsized influence that lobbies wield over the democratic process. The disproportionate power held by wealthy interests and the looming specter of corruption and undue influence have raised red flags about the integrity of our decision-making processes. As such, it is imperative for lobbies to conduct their activities with utmost transparency and ethical standards. Policymakers must also remain vigilant in considering a diverse array of viewpoints and interests in order to ensure fair and just decision-making.

Overall, lobbies can be a valuable and important part of a democratic system, but it is essential to ensure that they are accountable, transparent, and represent a broad range of voices in order to uphold the principles of democracy.

The list of the biggest Lobbies in USA and Europe

Some of the biggest lobbying organizations in the United States include:

1. U.S. Chamber of Commerce
2. National Association of Realtors
3. American Medical Association
4. Pharmaceutical Research and Manufacturers of America (PhRMA)
5. National Rifle Association (NRA)
6. American Hospital Association
7. American Petroleum Institute
8. National Association of Manufacturers
9. American Israel Public Affairs Committee (AIPAC)
10. National Education Association

In Europe, some of the biggest lobbying organizations include:

1. European Round Table of Industrialists
2. Confederation of British Industry (CBI)
3. BusinessEurope
4. European Federation of Pharmaceutical Industries and Associations (EFPIA)
5. European Automobile Manufacturers Association (ACEA)
6. European Banking Federation
7. European Chemical Industry Council (Cefic)
8. European Association of Automotive Suppliers (CLEPA)
9. European Association of Chambers of Commerce and Industry (EUROCHAMBRES)
10. European Public Health Alliance (EPHA)

The role of the freemasonry in the democratic contest

Freemasonry has historically played a role in shaping democratic principles and advocating for individual rights and freedoms. Freemasonry promotes values such as tolerance, equality, and fraternity, which are essential to the functioning of a democratic society.

In some countries, Freemasonry has been involved in political movements and has advocated for democratic reforms. For example, in the United States, many of the founding fathers were Freemasons and the principles of Freemasonry, such as the importance of individual liberty and equality, influenced the drafting of the Constitution.

However, it is important to note that Freemasonry is a non-political organization and does not officially endorse any political candidates or parties. Freemasonry is open to men of all backgrounds and beliefs, and members are encouraged to engage in civil discourse and respect differing opinions.

Overall, Freemasonry's role in the democratic contest is one of promoting democratic values and principles, rather than actively participating in political campaigns or elections. Its influence on democracy is more subtle and indirect, through the promotion of individual rights, tolerance, and equality.

The List of the most powerful freemasonry in USA and Europe

1. Grand Lodge of England (United Kingdom)
2. Grand Lodge of New York (USA)
3. Grand Orient de France (France)
4. United Grand Lodge of Germany (Germany)
5. Grand Lodge of Pennsylvania (USA)
6. Grand Lodge of California (USA)
7. Grand Lodge of Massachusetts (USA)
8. Grand Lodge of Ohio (USA)
9. Grand Lodge of Texas (USA)
10. Grand Lodge of Italy (Italy)

Can freemasonry be considered a type of lobbying?

No, Freemasonry is not a lobby. It is important to understand that Freemasonry is a longstanding fraternal organization that has been dedicated to promoting moral and ethical values, fostering brotherhood among its members, and engaging in various charitable efforts. It is crucial to note that Freemasonry does not engage in any lobbying activities or seek to exert political influence in any way.

Foreign capital and lobbying are disrupting democracy. For example:

One example of foreign capital and lobbies interfering with democracy is the case of Russian interference in the 2016 US presidential election. It was reported that Russia used social media platforms to spread disinformation and influence the outcome of the election in favor of then-candidate Donald Trump. This interference raised concerns about the integrity of the democratic process and the influence of foreign actors on domestic politics. Additionally, foreign lobbying groups have been known to influence policymakers and government decisions through financial contributions and other means, potentially undermining the will of the people and democratic principles.

Explaining the Role of Interest Groups in Democracy

Interest groups play a crucial role in a democracy by representing the interests and concerns of specific groups of people within society. These groups advocate for their members' interests by lobbying policymakers, engaging in public education campaigns, and mobilizing grassroots support.

Interest groups help to ensure that a diverse range of voices and perspectives are heard in the policymaking process, thereby contributing to a more inclusive and representative democracy. They provide a way for individuals to collectively organize and have their voices heard on issues that are important to them.

Furthermore, interest groups can serve as a check on government power by holding policymakers accountable and advocating for transparency and accountability in the decision-making process. By providing information and expertise on specific policy issues, interest groups can help policymakers make more informed decisions.

Overall, interest groups play an important role in strengthening democracy by promoting civic engagement, facilitating dialogue between different stakeholders, and ensuring that the diverse interests and concerns of society are considered in the policymaking process.

In a vibrant democracy, the voices of the people should be heard and their interests should be represented. However, the reality is often far from this ideal. This subchapter will delve into the concept of interest groups and explore their role in shaping democratic processes and outcomes.

Interest groups, also known as advocacy groups or pressure groups, are organizations that aim to influence public policy on behalf of specific interests. These groups can represent a wide range of stakeholders, including businesses, labor unions, professional associations, environmental organizations, and social justice movements. Their primary purpose is to advocate for the interests of their members and advance their policy goals.

The influence of interest groups on democratic decision-making is a topic of great importance and debate. On one hand, interest groups play a crucial role in a pluralistic democracy by providing a platform for diverse voices and ensuring that different perspectives are considered. They can provide expertise, research, and resources to inform policy debates. However, critics argue that the power of interest groups can undermine democratic principles, especially when certain groups have disproportionate access to policymakers or when their influence is driven by financial resources.

Examining the Types of Interest Groups and their Influence

Interest groups play a significant role in shaping public policy and influencing government decisions. There are several types of interest groups, each with their own objectives and methods of influence. Some of the most common types of interest groups include:

1. Economic interest groups: These groups represent the interests of businesses, industries, and trade associations. They often advocate for policies that benefit their members, such as tax breaks, deregulation, or trade agreements. Examples of economic interest groups include the U.S. Chamber of Commerce and the National Association of Manufacturers.
2. Labor interest groups: These groups represent the interests of workers and labor unions. They advocate for policies that protect workers' rights, promote fair wages, and improve working conditions. Examples of labor interest groups include the AFL-CIO and the United Auto Workers.
3. Environmental interest groups: These groups advocate for policies that protect the environment and promote sustainability. They often work to influence government decisions on issues such as climate change, pollution, and conservation. Examples of environmental interest groups include the Sierra Club and Greenpeace.
4. Public interest groups: These groups advocate for policies that benefit the general public or specific communities. They often focus on issues such as civil rights, healthcare, education, and consumer protection. Examples of public interest groups include the American Civil Liberties Union (ACLU) and the National Association for the Advancement of Colored People (NAACP).
5. Ideological interest groups: These groups advocate for policies based on a specific ideology or belief system. They may focus on issues such as gun rights, abortion, or immigration. Examples of ideological

interest groups include the National Rifle Association (NRA) and Planned Parenthood.

Interest groups use a variety of tactics to influence government decisions, including lobbying, campaign contributions, grassroots organizing, and litigation. They also play a key role in shaping public opinion through media campaigns and advocacy efforts.

Overall, interest groups can have a significant impact on the policy-making process and the decisions of government officials. By mobilizing their members and resources, interest groups are able to effectively advocate for their interests and shape the political landscape.

Interest groups play a crucial role in shaping political agendas and influencing democratic outcomes.

Interest groups, whether they are financial lobbies or grassroots movements, possess significant power in shaping political agendas. We will explore how interest groups mobilize resources, employ lobbying tactics, and utilize media platforms to influence public opinion and policy decisions. By understanding the power dynamics between interest groups and political institutions, we can assess the strengths and limitations of democratic governance.

Examining the types of interest groups and their influence is essential for democracy and political enthusiasts. By delving into topics such as financial lobbies, the role of money in politics, populism, and media influence, we can gain a comprehensive understanding of the dynamics shaping democratic outcomes. This subchapter aims to provide insights into the multifaceted nature of interest group influence and its significance in the fate of democracy.

Analyzing, describing and make categories the Strategies Employed by Interest Groups

Interest groups employ a variety of strategies to achieve their goals and influence public policy. These strategies can be categorized into several broad categories:

1. Lobbying: Lobbying is one of the most common strategies used by interest groups. This involves contacting policymakers, such as members of Congress, to advocate for specific policies or legislation that align with the group's interests. Lobbyists may meet with lawmakers, provide them with information and research, and try to persuade them to support the group's position.
2. Grassroots mobilization: Interest groups often mobilize their members and supporters to take action on specific issues. This can include organizing rallies, protests, letter-writing campaigns, or phone banks to put pressure on policymakers to support the group's agenda.
3. Campaign contributions: Interest groups may also make campaign contributions to candidates who support their positions. This can help ensure that policymakers are more likely to listen to the group's concerns and prioritize their issues.
4. Public relations and media campaigns: Interest groups may use media campaigns to raise awareness of their issues and shape public opinion. This can include advertising, op-eds, social media campaigns, and other efforts to influence public perception and support for the group's agenda.

5. Coalition-building: Interest groups may form coalitions with other organizations that share similar goals or interests. By working together, groups can amplify their voices and increase their influence on policymakers.
6. Legal strategies: Some interest groups may use legal strategies, such as filing lawsuits or participating in legal proceedings, to advance their goals. This can be a particularly effective strategy for groups seeking to challenge existing laws or regulations.

Overall, interest groups employ a combination of these strategies to advance their interests and influence public policy. The effectiveness of these strategies can vary depending on factors such as the resources of the group, the level of public support for their cause, and the political climate.

Interest groups play a significant role in shaping political agendas and influencing democratic outcomes. In this subchapter, we will delve into the strategies employed by interest groups, examining their impact on democracy and political decision-making.

Where do the major funds go for financing political parties or candidates during elections?

Big money for financing parties or candidates of elections typically comes from wealthy individuals, corporations, and special interest groups. This money can be donated directly to candidates or parties, or it can be funneled through political action committees (PACs) or super PACs, which can raise and spend unlimited amounts of money to support or oppose candidates.

Some of the biggest sources of campaign financing include:

1. Wealthy individuals: Billionaires and millionaires often donate large sums of money to political candidates and parties, either through direct contributions or by hosting fundraising events.
2. Corporations: Corporations can donate money to candidates and parties through their political action committees (PACs) or through independent expenditures.
3. Special interest groups: Groups representing specific industries or causes, such as labor unions, environmental organizations, and gun rights advocates, often spend significant amounts of money to support candidates who align with their interests.
4. Super PACs: Super PACs are independent political committees that can raise and spend unlimited amounts of money to support or oppose candidates, as long as they do not coordinate with the candidates' campaigns.

Overall, campaign financing in the United States is largely driven by big money interests, and critics argue that this system can lead to corruption and undue influence over the political process.

Who are the top 20 US and European billionaires that officially finance, support and help political parties and candidates in elections

It is crucial to acknowledge that the lack of transparency surrounding political donations and support from billionaires can make it challenging to accurately identify the top contributors. Despite this, there are several prominent billionaires who have been widely reported to provide financial backing to political parties and candidates in both the United States and Europe. Some of these well-known individuals include:

US billionaires:

1. Sheldon Adelson
2. Charles Koch
3. David Koch (deceased)
4. Michael Bloomberg
5. George Soros
6. Tom Steyer
7. Warren Buffett
8. Peter Thiel
9. Robert Mercer
10. Jeff Bezos
11. Mark Zuckerberg
12. Elon Musk
13. Larry Ellison
14. Jim Simons
15. Ray Dalio
16. Tim Gill
17. Steve Ballmer
18. Donald Sussman
19. Larry Page
20. Sergey Brin

European billionaires:

1. George Soros (also active in US politics)
2. Hansjörg Wyss
3. Bernard Arnault
4. Amancio Ortega
5. Stefan Persson
6. Serge Dassault
7. Susanne Klatten

8. Dieter Schwarz
9. Theo Albrecht Jr.
10. Thomas Peterffy
11. Ingvar Kamprad (deceased)
12. Stefano Pessina
13. Jacqueline Mars
14. John Mars
15. Andrey Melnichenko
16. Leonid Mikhelson
17. Vladimir Lisin
18. Alisher Usmanov
19. Mikhail Fridman
20. Roman Abramovich

Please note that this is not an exhaustive list and the political activities of billionaires may vary.

Investigating Lobbying Techniques and their Effectiveness

Lobbying is the act of attempting to influence decisions made by government officials on behalf of a specific organization or group. It is a common practice in politics and can have a significant impact on policy outcomes. There are several techniques that lobbyists use to influence decision-makers, including:

1. Building relationships: Lobbyists often build relationships with government officials through social interactions, networking events, and campaign contributions. These relationships can help lobbyists gain access to decision-makers and influence their decisions.

2. Providing information: Lobbyists provide decision-makers with information, data, and research to support their positions. This information can help decision-makers better understand the issues at hand and make informed decisions.
3. Mobilizing support: Lobbyists work to mobilize support for their cause by organizing grassroots campaigns, rallies, and letter-writing campaigns. This can create pressure on decision-makers to take action on the issues that lobbyists are advocating for.
4. Offering incentives: Lobbyists may offer incentives to decision-makers, such as campaign contributions, gifts, or job opportunities, in exchange for their support. While this practice is controversial and can be unethical, it is still commonly used in lobbying efforts.

The effectiveness of lobbying techniques can vary depending on the specific circumstances and context in which they are used. Some factors that can influence the effectiveness of lobbying efforts include the level of public support for the issue, the resources and expertise of the lobbying organization, and the political climate.

Overall, lobbying can be an effective tool for influencing policy outcomes, but it is important for lobbyists to be transparent, ethical, and strategic in their efforts. By using a combination of relationship-building, information-providing, mobilizing support, and offering incentives, lobbyists can increase their chances of successfully influencing decision-makers and achieving their policy goals.

Our goal is to promote informed discussions and spark potential reforms that strengthen the foundations of our democratic systems through a comprehensive analysis and transparency in democracy.

Assessing the Role of Grassroots Movements in Shaping Policies and make some exemple

Grassroots movements play a crucial role in shaping policies by mobilizing communities, raising awareness about important issues, and advocating for change from the ground up. These movements often start at the local level and gain momentum through grassroots organizing, activism, and advocacy efforts. Here are some examples of grassroots movements that have successfully influenced policies:

1. The civil rights movement in the United States was a grassroots movement that fought against racial segregation and discrimination. Through protests, marches, and advocacy campaigns, activists were able to bring attention to the injustices faced by African Americans and push for legislative changes, such as the Civil Rights Act of 1964 and the Voting Rights Act of 1965.
2. The environmental movement has also been driven by grassroots efforts to raise awareness about climate change, pollution, and conservation. Organizations like Greenpeace and the Sierra Club have mobilized communities to advocate for policies that protect the environment, such as the Clean Air Act and the Endangered Species Act.
3. The #MeToo movement, which started as a grassroots social media campaign, has sparked a global conversation about sexual harassment and assault. By sharing their stories and experiences, survivors have brought attention to the prevalence of gender-based violence and pushed for changes in workplace policies and cultural attitudes towards harassment.

In general, grassroots movements can influence policies by amplifying the voices of marginalized communities, ensuring policymakers are held accountable, and driving social change from the grassroots level. Through organizing, mobilizing, and advocating for their beliefs, grassroots movements are able to impact decision-makers and implement important policy changes. In the current political environment, grassroots movements have become a significant force in shaping policies and affecting democratic results. These movements, led by everyday citizens who are passionate about a cause, have consistently demonstrated their ability to challenge existing power structures and create real change.

In democracy, the question of true power - lobbies or people? Grassroots movements argue for the latter, countering corporate influence. Populism's rise impacts democracy, with grassroots leading the charge for accountability and policy change.

Interest groups, whether corporate or otherwise, have long played a significant role in shaping political agendas. However, grassroots movements have demonstrated their ability to challenge and disrupt this power dynamic. By organizing protests, advocating for policy changes, and leveraging the power of social media, grassroots movements have forced politicians to pay attention and address the issues that matter to the people.

In conclusion, grassroots movements have become an integral part of democratic processes, challenging established power structures, and shaping policies. Their ability to mobilize citizens, raise awareness, and demand change has proven to be a powerful force in driving democratic outcomes. As democracy and political lovers, it is essential for us to recognize and support the role of grassroots movements in shaping policies and ensuring that the voice of the people is heard and respected.

Assessing the Impact of Interest Groups on Democratic Decision-Making

In the contemporary political landscape, the influence of interest groups on democratic decision-making has become a subject of intense scrutiny and debate. In this subchapter, we will delve into the complex dynamics between interest groups and democracy, examining the various ways in which they shape political agendas and impact democratic outcomes.

Interest groups play a significant role in influencing democratic decision-making processes. They represent the interests of specific groups of individuals or organizations and advocate for policies that align with those interests. While interest groups can provide valuable expertise and information to policymakers, they can also have a negative impact on democratic decision-making.

One of the main ways interest groups influence democratic decision-making is through lobbying. Interest groups often have access to policymakers and can use their resources to influence legislation and policy decisions. This can lead to policies that primarily benefit the interests of the group, rather than the broader public interest.

Additionally, interest groups can also shape public opinion and mobilize support for their causes. Through advertising campaigns, grassroots organizing, and media outreach, interest groups can sway public opinion and put pressure on policymakers to align with their interests.

However, the influence of interest groups can also have negative consequences for democratic decision-making. Interest groups with more resources and power may have a disproportionate influence on policy decisions, leading to policies that benefit the wealthy and powerful at the expense of marginalized communities.

Furthermore, the influence of interest groups can also lead to a lack of transparency and accountability in the decision-making process. When policymakers are heavily influenced by interest groups, it can be difficult for the public to understand who is truly shaping policy decisions and hold decision-makers accountable.

In conclusion, interest groups play a significant role in democratic decision-making processes. While they can provide valuable expertise and advocacy on important issues, their influence can also have negative consequences for democracy. It is important for policymakers to be vigilant about the influence of interest groups and ensure that decisions are made in the best interests of the public as a whole.

By examining these critical aspects of interest group influence on democratic decision-making, we aim to provide a comprehensive understanding of the challenges and opportunities that arise in the pursuit of a truly democratic society. This subchapter will be of interest to democracy and political lovers who seek to comprehend the nuanced relationship between interest groups, democratic institutions, and the fate of democracy itself.

Exploring the Influence of Interest Groups on Policy Formation

Interest groups play a significant role in shaping policy formation by advocating for their specific interests and influencing decision-makers. These groups represent a variety of stakeholders, including businesses, labor unions, advocacy organizations, and other entities with a vested interest in particular policy outcomes. Interest groups engage in various tactics to influence policy formation, such as lobbying, providing campaign contributions, conducting research, and mobilizing public support.

One way interest groups influence policy formation is through lobbying. Lobbying involves direct communication with policymakers to advocate for specific policies or legislation that align with the interests of the group. Interest groups often hire lobbyists to represent their interests and communicate with lawmakers on their behalf. Lobbyists may provide policymakers with information, research, and data to support their positions and persuade them to adopt policies favorable to the group.

Interest groups also influence policy formation through campaign contributions. By donating money to political candidates and parties, interest groups can gain access and influence over decision-makers. Campaign contributions can help interest groups build relationships with policymakers and ensure that their interests are considered when shaping policy.

Another way interest groups influence policy formation is by conducting research and providing expertise on relevant issues. Interest groups often produce reports, studies, and analysis to support their positions and provide policymakers with data-driven evidence to inform their decision-making. By providing policymakers with credible information and expertise, interest groups can shape the policy debate and influence the direction of policy formation.

Additionally, interest groups mobilize public support to influence policy formation. By organizing grassroots campaigns, rallies, and advocacy efforts, interest groups can generate public awareness and pressure policymakers to take action on specific issues. Public support can help interest groups build momentum and create a sense of urgency around their policy priorities, increasing the likelihood of policy changes in their favor.

Overall, interest groups play a crucial role in shaping policy formation by advocating for their specific interests, engaging in lobbying and advocacy efforts, providing expertise and research, and mobilizing public support. By leveraging their resources and influence, interest groups can effectively shape policy outcomes and influence decision-makers to adopt policies that align with their interests.

Interest groups, also known as pressure groups or advocacy organizations, play a crucial role in shaping political agendas. They represent the interests of specific sectors or communities, wielding their influence to sway policy decisions in their favor. However, the question that arises is whether this influence aligns with the principles of a true democracy.

In this context, interest groups exert their power to shape political agendas and influence policy outcomes. Their ability to mobilize resources, organize grassroots campaigns, and influence public opinion through media channels cannot be underestimated. The role of media in shaping democratic outcomes cannot be overlooked either. Media platforms play a crucial role in disseminating information, framing public debates, and shaping public opinion. The relationship between media, interest groups, and the fate of democracy is closely intertwined, with both positive and negative implications.

To understand the influence of interest groups on policy formation, it is essential to analyze the interplay between real democracy, corporate lobbies, money in politics, populism, media, and democratic outcomes. By critically examining these factors, we can strive for a better understanding of the challenges and opportunities that lie ahead in our pursuit of a more inclusive and vibrant democracy.

Evaluating the Balance between Interest Group Influence and Democratic Representation

Interest groups play a significant role in influencing government decisions and policies, but their influence must be balanced with the principles of democratic representation to ensure that the interests of all citizens are taken into account.

On one hand, interest groups provide valuable input and expertise on specific issues, allowing policymakers to make more informed decisions. They also help to amplify the voices of marginalized or underrepresented groups, ensuring that their concerns are not overlooked.

However, interest groups can also exert undue influence on the political process, particularly when they have significant financial resources or are able to mobilize large numbers of supporters. This can lead to policies that primarily benefit the interests of a few powerful groups, rather than the broader public interest.

To maintain a balance between interest group influence and democratic representation, policymakers should be transparent about their interactions with interest groups and ensure that a diverse range of perspectives are considered in the decision-making process. It is also important to strengthen campaign finance regulations to prevent undue influence from wealthy interest groups.

Ultimately, the goal should be to create a political system that is responsive to the needs and preferences of all citizens, rather than just a select few. Striking the right balance between interest group influence and democratic representation is essential for achieving this goal.

Here we aim to provide democracy and political lovers with a comprehensive understanding of the intricate dynamics between interest group influence and democratic representation. We aim to examine how corporate lobbies, money in politics, populism, and interest groups impact our democracy, in order to understand the challenges we face and explore ways to restore a balance between interest group influence and democratic representation.

Chapter 4: The Role of Media and its Influence on Democratic Outcomes

Understanding the Role of Media in Democracy

Media plays a crucial role in democracy by providing information and acting as a watchdog to hold those in power accountable. Here are some key aspects of the role of media in democracy:

1. Informing the public: Media outlets provide citizens with information about current events, government policies, and issues that affect their lives. This helps to ensure that citizens are informed and able to make educated decisions when voting or participating in public debates.
2. Acting as a watchdog: Media serves as a check on government power by investigating and reporting on corruption, abuse of power, and other wrongdoing by public officials. This helps to hold those in power accountable and prevent the abuse of power.
3. Promoting public debate: Media outlets provide a platform for different viewpoints and opinions to be heard, fostering public debate and discussion on important issues. This helps to ensure that a variety of perspectives are considered in decision-making processes.
4. Advocating for transparency and accountability: Media plays a key role in advocating for transparency in government and holding public officials accountable for their actions. By shining a light on government activities, media helps to ensure that government operates in the public interest.
5. Educating and empowering citizens: Media outlets educate citizens about their rights, responsibilities, and the workings of government,

empowering them to participate in democratic processes and hold their leaders accountable.

Overall, a free and independent media is essential for the functioning of a healthy democracy. By providing information, acting as a watchdog, promoting public debate, advocating for transparency and accountability, and empowering citizens, media plays a vital role in ensuring that government is responsive to the needs and interests of the people.

Defining Media's Role as the Fourth Estate in the context of Freedom of speech, Freedom of press and Freedom of information.

The Fourth Estate refers to the role of the media in society as a watchdog and guardian of democracy. In a democratic society, the media plays a crucial role in holding those in power accountable, providing information to the public, and acting as a check on government actions.

Freedom of speech, freedom of the press, and freedom of information are fundamental rights that are essential for a functioning democracy. These rights allow individuals to express their opinions, access information, and hold those in power accountable without fear of censorship or retaliation.

The media's role as the Fourth Estate is closely tied to these freedoms, as journalists and news organizations rely on them to fulfill their duty to inform the public and act as a watchdog. Without freedom of speech, press, and information, the media would not be able to fulfill its role as an independent and critical voice in society.

In essence, the media's role as the Fourth Estate is contingent upon the protection of these freedoms, as they are essential for ensuring a free and vibrant press that can serve as a check on government power and promote transparency and accountability in society. When these freedoms are threatened or undermined, the media's ability to act as the Fourth Estate is compromised, potentially leading to a weakening of democratic institutions and a loss of public trust in the media.

What causes the influence of the big brother effect on modern democracy: Media, propaganda, or brainwashing?

The "Big Brother effect" in modern democracy refers to the idea of a powerful entity, such as the government or media, exerting control over the thoughts and actions of individuals. This can take the form of propaganda, manipulation of information, or psychological manipulation to influence public opinion and behavior.

In a democratic society, the Big Brother effect can be seen as a threat to individual freedom and autonomy. It is crucial to recognize that the manipulation of information can distort the opinions and decisions of citizens, leading them to support policies or candidates that may not reflect their genuine beliefs and values. This distortion of the democratic process can have far-reaching consequences, weakening the foundations of freedom of speech and expression that are essential for a functioning democracy. It is imperative that safeguards are put in place to protect the integrity of the democratic system and ensure that citizens are able to make informed choices based on accurate and unbiased information.

It is crucial for individuals to be highly discerning and thoughtful consumers of media and information, actively making the effort to access a wide array of sources for news and differing viewpoints. By remaining informed, consistently questioning the narratives being fed to them, and cultivating a healthy skepticism towards the information they encounter, individuals can effectively combat the pervasive influence of the Big Brother effect. In doing so, they are not only safeguarding their democratic rights and freedoms but also actively participating in the preservation of a truly informed and empowered society.

Analyzing the Functions of Media in Facilitating Democratic Discourse

Media plays a crucial role in facilitating democratic discourse by providing a platform for the exchange of ideas, opinions, and information among citizens. Here are some key functions of media in this regard:

1. Information dissemination: Media outlets, such as newspapers, television, radio, and online platforms, serve as channels for providing citizens with essential information about public affairs, government policies, current events, and social issues. This helps to keep the public informed and engaged in the democratic process.
2. Public debate and discussion: Media platforms allow for the expression of diverse viewpoints and opinions on various topics, fostering healthy public debate and discussion. This enables citizens to critically evaluate different perspectives and make informed decisions on important issues.
3. Holding the government accountable: Through investigative journalism and reporting, the media acts as a watchdog to hold government officials and institutions accountable for their actions and decisions. This helps to ensure transparency, accountability, and integrity in the democratic system.
4. Representation of diverse voices: Media outlets provide a platform for marginalized and underrepresented groups to have their voices heard in the public discourse. This promotes inclusivity, diversity, and equity in democratic decision-making processes.
5. Educating the public: Media plays a crucial role in educating the public about democratic principles, rights, and responsibilities. This helps to empower citizens to participate effectively in the democratic process and make informed decisions about their governance.
6. Mobilizing public opinion: Media can influence public opinion and shape attitudes towards political issues and candidates. By framing

and presenting information in a certain way, the media can mobilize public opinion and drive social and political change.

Overall, the media's functions in facilitating democratic discourse are essential for promoting a vibrant, informed, and participatory democracy. It is important for media outlets to uphold ethical standards, promote diversity of voices, and provide accurate and unbiased information to effectively serve this role.

In today's digital age, the media plays a pivotal role in facilitating democratic discourse. It serves as a platform for citizens to engage in conversations, exchange diverse viewpoints, and hold those in power accountable.

Furthermore, the role of money in politics cannot be overlooked. The infusion of money into political campaigns and elections can greatly impact democratic processes. Media plays a vital role in uncovering the sources of campaign funding and highlighting the potential conflicts of interest that may arise. By providing transparency and information on financial contributions, media outlets empower citizens to make informed decisions and question the influence of money on democratic outcomes.

Who are the owner of the big US and European Group and the connection with politics. 20 Exemples

1. The Koch brothers, Charles and David Koch, own a large US conglomerate with interests in various industries such as energy, chemicals, and manufacturing. They have been known to financially support conservative political causes and candidates.
2. George Soros, a billionaire investor, is the owner of a European group with diverse holdings in finance, media, and technology. He is also a prominent donor to liberal and progressive political causes and organizations.
3. Rupert Murdoch, chairman of News Corp, owns a major media conglomerate with holdings in both the US and Europe. His media outlets have been accused of having a conservative bias and influencing politics through their reporting.
4. The Walton family, owners of Walmart, have a significant impact on US politics due to their wealth and influence. They have been known to support Republican candidates and causes.
5. Carlos Slim, a Mexican billionaire, owns a large European telecom group with investments in telecommunications and infrastructure. He has been involved in politics in Mexico and has close ties to the country's political elite.
6. Mark Zuckerberg, CEO of Facebook, owns a major tech company with a global reach. Facebook has faced criticism for its role in influencing politics and elections through its platform.
7. Jeff Bezos, CEO of Amazon, owns a major e-commerce and tech company with significant influence in the US and Europe. His ownership of The Washington Post has also raised questions about media and politics.

8. Warren Buffett, CEO of Berkshire Hathaway, owns a diverse conglomerate with interests in insurance, energy, and consumer goods. He is known for his philanthropy and has been involved in politics through his advocacy for higher taxes on the wealthy.
9. Larry Page and Sergey Brin, co-founders of Google, own a major tech company with a global presence. Google's algorithms and search results have been accused of influencing politics and elections.
10. The Hearst family, owners of Hearst Corporation, have a major media presence in the US and Europe. Their ownership of newspapers, magazines, and TV stations has led to accusations of political bias and influence.

Keep in mind that the media is crucial for providing information, allowing people to access diverse perspectives, participate in discussions, and make well-informed choices. It also acts as a watchdog, holding those in power accountable for their actions. This section will explore how the media supports democratic discussions, highlighting the significance of a free and independent media for a strong democracy. In summary, the media's roles in promoting democratic conversations are varied and crucial for a thriving democracy. Whether it's uncovering corporate influences, examining the impact of money in politics, or challenging the spread of populism, the media is essential for empowering citizens and safeguarding democratic processes. This section will offer a thorough examination of how the media influences democratic outcomes, addressing the concerns of democracy advocates, political enthusiasts, and those worried about the influence of interest groups and corporations on democratic decision-making.

Examining the Influence of Media Ownership and Control

Media ownership and control play a significant role in shaping the content and messages that are disseminated to the public. The consolidation of media ownership in the hands of a few conglomerates has raised concerns about the potential for bias, censorship, and limited diversity of viewpoints in the media landscape.

One of the key concerns related to media ownership is the potential for bias and lack of objectivity in reporting. When a small number of companies control a large portion of the media market, there is a risk that the interests and agendas of these companies will influence the content that is produced and distributed. This can lead to a limited range of perspectives being presented to the public, and can result in the suppression of dissenting voices or alternative viewpoints.

Another issue related to media ownership is the potential for censorship and self-censorship. When media outlets are owned by a small number of companies, there is a risk that certain topics or viewpoints may be suppressed in order to protect the interests of the owners or to maintain good relationships with advertisers or government officials. This can result in a narrowing of the public discourse and a limitation of the information available to the public.

Furthermore, media ownership can also impact the diversity of voices and perspectives that are represented in the media. When a small number of companies control a large portion of the media market, there is a risk that certain viewpoints or communities may be marginalized or excluded from the public conversation. This can lead to a lack of representation for minority groups, and can perpetuate stereotypes and biases in the media.

Overall, the influence of media ownership and control on the content and messages that are disseminated to the public is a complex and multifaceted issue. It is important for policymakers, regulators, and media consumers to be aware of the potential risks and challenges associated with concentrated media ownership, and to work towards promoting a diverse and inclusive media landscape that reflects the full range of perspectives and voices in society.

Understanding the influence of media ownership and control is crucial for anyone passionate about democracy and politics. This subchapter delves deep into the intricate dynamics between media ownership, corporate lobbies, populism, and the fate of democracy.

Investigating the Impact of Corporate Media Ownership on Democratic Reporting

Corporate media ownership has a significant impact on the type of reporting that is produced and disseminated to the public. When a small number of corporations own a large portion of the media outlets, there is a risk that the reporting may be biased or skewed to serve the interests of the owners rather than providing objective and balanced coverage.

One of the main concerns with corporate media ownership is the potential for conflicts of interest to arise. If a media company is owned by a large corporation, there may be pressure to prioritize stories that are favorable to the corporate interests or to avoid reporting on topics that could be detrimental to the owners. This can result in a lack of diversity in the perspectives and viewpoints presented in the media, which is essential for a healthy democratic society.

Furthermore, corporate media ownership can also lead to a concentration of power in the hands of a few individuals or entities. This can limit the range of voices that are heard in the media and stifle independent and critical reporting. It can also result in a homogenization of news content, with stories being framed in a way that aligns with the interests of the owners.

In order to counteract the negative effects of corporate media ownership on democratic reporting, it is important for media outlets to uphold journalistic ethics and standards of objectivity and impartiality. Additionally, there should be regulations in place to promote media diversity and prevent monopolies in the media industry. Independent media watchdogs and organizations can also play a crucial role in holding media outlets accountable and ensuring that they serve the public interest.

Overall, the impact of corporate media ownership on democratic reporting is a complex and multifaceted issue that requires careful consideration and ongoing monitoring. By promoting transparency, diversity, and accountability in the media industry, we can help to safeguard the integrity of journalism and ensure that the public has access to accurate and unbiased information.

By investigating the impact of corporate media ownership on democratic reporting, this subchapter aims to shed light on the complexities of the media landscape and its implications for democratic processes. It encourages readers, particularly democracy and political enthusiasts, to critically evaluate the role of media and its influence on shaping the fate of democracy in an increasingly interconnected world.

Assessing the Role of State-Owned Media in Shaping Public Opinion

State-owned media plays a significant role in shaping public opinion as it is often used by governments to promote their agendas, control the flow of information, and influence public perception. While state-owned media can provide a platform for government propaganda and biased reporting, it can also serve as a tool for disseminating important information and shaping public discourse.

One of the key ways in which state-owned media can influence public opinion is through selective reporting and censorship. Governments can use state-owned media to control the narrative and shape public perception by highlighting certain stories and viewpoints while downplaying or ignoring others. This can lead to a skewed presentation of information and limit the public's access to diverse perspectives.

State-owned media can also be used to promote government policies and initiatives, shaping public opinion by framing issues in a favorable light. By controlling the messaging and framing of news stories, state-owned media can influence public perception and support for government actions.

Additionally, state-owned media can play a role in shaping public opinion through propaganda and misinformation. Governments can use state-owned media to spread false or misleading information in order to manipulate public opinion and advance their agendas. This can have a significant impact on public perception and trust in the media.

On the other hand, state-owned media can also serve as a source of reliable information and news for the public. In some cases, state-owned media outlets may provide important news coverage and analysis that is not available from other sources. This can help to inform the public and shape public discourse on important issues.

Overall, the role of state-owned media in shaping public opinion is complex and multifaceted. While it can be used by governments to promote their agendas and control the flow of information, state-owned media can also serve as a valuable source of news and analysis for the public. It is important for individuals to critically evaluate the information they receive from state-owned media and seek out diverse sources of news and information in order to form a well-rounded understanding of issues.

One of the key debates surrounding state-owned media is the extent to which they can present unbiased and objective information. Critics argue that these media outlets often serve as propaganda machines, promoting the government's agenda and suppressing dissenting voices. This raises concerns about the integrity of democratic processes and the ability of citizens to make informed decisions.

On the other hand, proponents argue that state-owned media can provide a counterbalance to corporate media, which is often influenced by powerful interest groups. They suggest that state-owned media can prioritize the public interest and provide a platform for marginalized voices that may not have access to corporate media.

To assess the role of state-owned media in shaping public opinion, it is important to consider the context in which they operate. In some countries, state-owned media may be the only source of news and information available to citizens, making their influence even more significant. In such cases, it becomes crucial to ensure that state-owned media uphold journalistic standards, maintain editorial independence, and provide a plurality of voices.

Additionally, the rise of populism adds another layer of complexity to this discussion. Populist leaders often seek to control media narratives and use state-owned media as a tool to advance their populist agenda. This raises concerns about the erosion of democratic norms and the potential for the manipulation of public opinion.

To safeguard democracy and ensure that state-owned media serves the public interest, it is imperative to have robust mechanisms in place. These may include independent media regulators, transparent funding models, editorial charters, and safeguards against political interference.

In summary, it is important to analyze the impact of state-owned media on influencing public opinion in order to grasp the complexities of democracy. Are we at risk of falling victim to propaganda? Although state-owned media can offer a different perspective from corporate media and elevate marginalized voices, there are valid concerns about propaganda and the potential manipulation of public opinion. Finding a middle ground between serving the public interest and maintaining editorial independence is crucial to protect democratic principles and results.

Analyzing the Effects of the Media included TV Bias and Manipulation

The media plays a significant role in shaping public opinion and influencing political discourse. However, the media is not always impartial and can exhibit bias and manipulation, particularly in the case of TV news.

TV bias refers to the tendency of news outlets to favor certain perspectives or ideologies over others. This can manifest in the selection of stories, the framing of issues, and the portrayal of individuals or groups. Bias can be subtle, such as through the use of language or imagery that subtly shapes viewers' perceptions, or more overt, such as through the deliberate omission of key information or the promotion of a particular agenda.

Manipulation in the media refers to the intentional distortion of information or events in order to influence public opinion or advance a particular agenda. This can take many forms, including the selective editing of footage, the use of misleading headlines or graphics, or the dissemination of false or misleading information. Manipulation can also involve the shaping of narratives or the promotion of particular ideas or values.

The effects of TV bias and manipulation can be significant. They can shape public opinion, reinforce existing beliefs, and influence political decision-making. They can also contribute to polarization and division within society, as viewers are exposed to a limited range of perspectives and are less likely to engage with opposing viewpoints.

In order to mitigate the effects of bias and manipulation in the media, it is important for viewers to be critical consumers of information. This means being aware of the potential for bias, seeking out a diverse range of sources, and critically evaluating the information presented. It also means holding media outlets accountable for their reporting and demanding transparency and accuracy in their coverage. Ultimately, a well-informed and engaged public is essential for a healthy democracy and a media landscape that serves the public interest.

Analyzing the Effects of social Media Bias and Manipulation

Social media bias and manipulation can have significant effects on society, politics, and public opinion. Here are some key ways in which bias and manipulation on social media can impact individuals and society as a whole:

1. Polarization: Social media platforms can amplify existing divisions and polarize society by promoting extreme viewpoints and limiting exposure to diverse perspectives. This can lead to echo chambers where users only see content that reinforces their existing beliefs, further entrenching divisions.
2. Disinformation: Social media platforms can be used to spread false information and propaganda, leading to the proliferation of fake news and misinformation. This can undermine trust in institutions, distort public debate, and manipulate public opinion.
3. Manipulation of elections: Social media platforms have been used to influence political elections through targeted advertising, misinformation campaigns, and the spread of divisive content. This can undermine the integrity of democratic processes and erode trust in the political system.
4. Amplification of hate speech: Social media platforms can be used to amplify hate speech, incite violence, and spread harmful ideologies. This can contribute to the radicalization of individuals and the proliferation of extremist views.
5. Personalized content: Social media algorithms can tailor content to individual users based on their preferences and browsing history, creating filter bubbles and reinforcing existing biases. This can limit exposure to diverse viewpoints and hinder critical thinking.

Social media bias and manipulation can have extensive and lasting impacts on individuals, communities, and society as a whole, influencing opinions, behaviors, and even political outcomes. Therefore, it is crucial for users to engage in critical thinking when consuming content on social media platforms, questioning sources and verifying information to combat the spread of misinformation. Additionally, it is imperative for social media companies to proactively implement measures to detect and eliminate bias and manipulation, ensuring a more transparent, trustworthy, and inclusive online space that promotes informed discourse and healthy communication.

Exploring the Ethical Challenges Faced by Journalists in Democracy

Journalists play a crucial role in a democracy by informing the public and holding those in power accountable. However, they also face a number of ethical challenges in their work. Some of the key ethical challenges faced by journalists in a democracy include:

1. Objectivity and bias: Journalists are expected to report the news objectively and without bias. However, it can be difficult to separate personal beliefs and opinions from their reporting. This can lead to biased or one-sided coverage of events, which can undermine the public's trust in the media.
2. Conflict of interest: Journalists may also face conflicts of interest in their reporting, especially if they have personal or financial ties to the subjects they are covering. This can compromise their ability to report the news accurately and impartially.
3. Sensationalism and clickbait: In an increasingly competitive media landscape, journalists may be tempted to resort to sensationalist or clickbait headlines to attract readers or viewers. This can distort the news and prioritize entertainment value over accuracy and relevance.

4. Privacy and intrusion: Journalists often have to balance the public's right to know with an individual's right to privacy. They may be tempted to intrude on people's personal lives in pursuit of a story, which can have harmful consequences for the individuals involved.
5. Fake news and misinformation: The rise of social media and online news sources has made it easier for fake news and misinformation to spread. Journalists have a responsibility to verify information before publishing it, but the pressure to be the first to break a story can sometimes lead to errors or inaccuracies.
6. Safety and security: Journalists around the world face physical and emotional risks in their work, especially in conflict zones or authoritarian regimes where press freedom is limited. They may be subject to harassment, censorship, or even violence for reporting on sensitive or controversial issues.

In conclusion, journalists in a democracy face a range of ethical challenges in their work, from maintaining objectivity and avoiding bias to navigating conflicts of interest and ensuring the accuracy of their reporting. It is crucial for journalists to uphold ethical standards and values in order to maintain the public's trust and credibility in the media.

So journalists play a crucial role in upholding the principles of democracy. They act as the watchdogs, ensuring transparency, accountability, and the dissemination of accurate information to the public. However, the ethical challenges faced by journalists in a democratic society are numerous and complex.

One of the key ethical challenges faced by journalists is navigating the influence of corporate lobbies on democratic decision-making. In a democracy, the interests of the people should take precedence over the interests of corporations. However, powerful corporate lobbies often exert significant influence over political decisions, creating a conflict of interest for journalists. They must weigh the importance of reporting facts against the pressure to appease powerful entities.

Money has a profound impact on democratic processes, from campaign financing to lobbying efforts. Journalists face the dilemma of reporting on the influence of money without compromising their own financial interests or succumbing to the pressures of sensationalism.

Populist movements often thrive on divisive rhetoric, misinformation, and the denigration of established institutions. Journalists must navigate the delicate balance between reporting on these movements objectively while ensuring they do not inadvertently amplify their harmful effects on democracy.

The power of interest groups in shaping political agendas is also a significant ethical challenge for journalists. These groups often have well-funded campaigns aimed at pushing their particular agenda. Journalists must remain vigilant in their reporting, ensuring they provide balanced coverage that represents the diverse perspectives of society, rather than becoming mouthpieces for specific interest groups.

The crucial role of media and its impact on democratic outcomes cannot be ignored. It is imperative for journalists to uphold the duty of delivering truthful and impartial information to the public, all the while recognizing the dangers of media manipulation and propaganda. It is essential for them to uphold their independence and combat the temptations of sensationalism and bias.

Journalists face numerous ethical challenges in a democratic society. The influence of corporate lobbies, the role of money in politics, the rise of populism, the power of interest groups, and the responsibility of media all contribute to the complexities of their profession.

However, it is through their dedication to the principles of democracy, their commitment to providing accurate and unbiased information, and their resilience in the face of these challenges that journalists can continue to shape the fate of democracy. It is imperative that journalists uphold the values of transparency, integrity, and accountability in order to maintain the trust of the public and hold those in power accountable. By staying true to their mission of informing the public and serving as watchdogs for democracy, journalists play a crucial role in safeguarding the democratic process and ensuring a well-informed citizenry. In a world filled with misinformation and propaganda, the importance of ethical journalism cannot be overstated.

Evaluating the Role of Fake News and Disinformation in Democratic Processes

Fake news and disinformation can have a significant impact on democratic processes by spreading false or misleading information that can influence public opinion, shape political discourse, and even sway election outcomes. In recent years, the rise of social media platforms has made it easier for fake news to spread rapidly and reach a wide audience, making it a growing concern for democratic societies.

One of the key ways in which fake news and disinformation can affect democratic processes is by undermining the public's trust in the media and institutions. When people are exposed to false information that is presented as fact, it can lead to confusion and skepticism about the credibility of news sources and political leaders. This can erode the foundation of a healthy democracy, which relies on an informed and engaged citizenry.

Additionally, fake news and disinformation can be used as a tool for political manipulation and propaganda. By spreading false information about political opponents or issues, individuals or groups can manipulate public opinion and sway election outcomes in their favor. This can distort the democratic process and undermine the integrity of elections.

In response to the growing threat of fake news and disinformation, many governments and tech companies have taken steps to combat the spread of false information online. This includes fact-checking initiatives, algorithm changes to reduce the visibility of fake news, and increased transparency around political advertising. However, the issue remains complex and ongoing, requiring continued vigilance and collaboration from all stakeholders involved in democratic processes.

Overall, the role of fake news and disinformation in democratic processes is a significant and evolving challenge that requires attention and action to protect the integrity of democratic institutions and ensure that citizens are able to make informed decisions. By addressing the spread of fake news and promoting media literacy, we can help safeguard the health of our democracies and ensure that the public has access to accurate and reliable information.

As democracy and political lovers, it is crucial for us to understand the various factors that shape the fate of our democracy, and the role of fake news and disinformation cannot be ignored.

Chapter 5: The political interference of foreign countries and its Effects on Democracy

Understanding how technology can be used to interfere in political life.

Foreign countries can interfere in the political life of other nations through various means, including the use of technology. Here are some of the commonly used technological tools for political interference:

Social media manipulation has become a pervasive issue in today's digital landscape. Alarmingly, foreign actors consistently exploit the wide reach of social media platforms as a means to spread disinformation, propaganda, and unfounded fake news. These malicious actors are cunningly adept at creating an array of fake accounts, groups, and pages, ingeniously designed to amplify select narratives, polarize entire societies, and deceitfully manipulate public opinion, thereby sowing the seeds of discord and mistrust.

1. Hacking and cyber attacks: In the realm of cybersecurity, state-sponsored hackers are relentlessly focusing their efforts on targeting not only political parties, government agencies, and election infrastructure, but also aiming for unauthorized access, slyly attempting to steal highly sensitive information, and cunningly disrupting crucial operations. These nefarious actors possess the ability to exploit compromised data by leaking compromising

information or subtly manipulating crucial data, ultimately aiming to significantly influence public perception and ultimately sway election outcomes.
2. Election interference: In today's digital age, foreign countries have the potential to exploit advanced technologies in order to interfere with crucial electoral processes. These nefarious activities encompass a range of destructive actions, such as surreptitiously infiltrating voter registration databases, disseminating pervasive disinformation campaigns targeting candidates or voting procedures, or even orchestrating sophisticated cyberattacks aimed at disrupting the entire voting process itself.
3. Surveillance and espionage: In an increasingly interconnected world, it has become evident that foreign governments have a propensity to employ an array of technologically advanced surveillance systems and espionage tactics in order to closely monitor and keep tabs on political opponents, activists, and even journalists who dare to speak truth to power. These insidious techniques go beyond mere eavesdropping, as they involve the interception of confidential communications, meticulous tracking of online activities, and the comprehensive collection of highly sensitive personal data with the sole purpose of acquiring an unfair advantage or exerting control over the fundamental democratic processes that shape the very fabric of our societies.
4. Propaganda campaigns, fueled by the advancements in technology, have granted foreign actors the ability to extensively disseminate propaganda and cunningly manipulate public opinion by fabricating and diligently promoting biased or entirely false narratives. This insidious act can be effectively executed through the implementation of highly targeted advertising strategies, strategically sponsored content, or even through the insidious creation and circulation of numerous deceptive fake news websites, cleverly designed to deceive and manipulate unsuspecting individuals.

1. Financial influence: In addition to its myriad applications, technology harnesses the power to skillfully manipulate intricate financial systems and, albeit indirectly, exert a profound impact on political

processes. Notably, foreign nations may actively contribute substantial funds to specific political parties or candidates, extend unwavering support to lobbying endeavors, or resort to the formidable tool of economic coercion, all in relentless pursuit of their coveted outcomes.

The ramifications of technological interference on democracy are of considerable magnitude. It serves to undermine the very essence of elections, corroding the bedrock of trust in democratic institutions, and fostering societal polarization. Additionally, it has the potential to stifle dissent, muzzle critical voices, and gradually erode the cherished principles of freedom of speech and expression. Counteracting and ameliorating these interferences necessitate a comprehensive approach encompassing international collaboration, enhanced cybersecurity protocols, educational endeavors to promote media literacy, and the establishment of robust legal frameworks.

The overwhelming influence of corporate lobbies on democratic decision-making raises concerns among both scholars and citizens. The role of money in politics and its impact on democratic processes cannot be ignored. We have personally witnessed how corporate influence has resulted in policies that benefit a privileged few at the expense of the majority, prompting urgent questions about the fairness, equity, and legitimacy of our democratic systems.

Simultaneously, the rise of populism has disrupted traditional political dynamics. Populist movements tap into people's disillusionment and grievances, promising to restore power to the masses. However, populism also carries risks for democracy, with its divisive rhetoric, exclusionary policies, and disregard for democratic principles.

Throughout our meticulously researched book, we emphasize the power and influence of interest groups in shaping political agendas. Whether they represent corporate interests or populist movements, these groups possess the ability to sway policy decisions and impact democratic governance. Therefore, understanding their role becomes crucial in safeguarding democratic processes.

Furthermore, our book examines the crucial role of media and its influence on democratic outcomes. Media has the power to shape public opinion, set the political agenda, and hold those in power accountable. However, media faces challenges in the digital age, including misinformation, echo chambers, and the erosion of trust in traditional sources.

As advocates for democracy, we must critically analyze these issues and strive to strengthen democratic institutions. We must ensure that political finance lobbies do not undermine the democratic will. At the same time, we must address the legitimate concerns that fuel the rise of populism in our societies.

To secure a prosperous future for democracy, we must champion transparency, accountability, and active civic participation. This necessitates implementing reforms to limit the influence of money in politics, supporting an independent media that truthfully informs the public, and nurturing an informed and engaged citizenry. Through these efforts, we can confront the challenges posed by the media-driven era and the rise of populism. Ultimately, we can build an enduring, inclusive, and thriving democracy that inspires future generations.

Chapter 6: The Revolution Will Be Televised: Media, Populism, and the Fate of Democracy

The Revolution Will Be Televised: Media, Populism, and the Fate of Democracy

As technology continues to advance and media outlets become more prevalent, the way in which information is disseminated and consumed has changed dramatically. This has had a profound impact on the way in which political movements and ideas are spread, leading to the rise of populism in many countries around the world.

In "The Revolution Will Be Televised: Media, Populism, and the Fate of Democracy," author examines the role that media plays in shaping public opinion and fueling populist movements. He argues that the proliferation of media outlets has led to a fragmentation of information, making it easier for individuals to seek out only the sources that align with their existing beliefs.

This has created echo chambers in which individuals are only exposed to information that reinforces their own views, leading to increased polarization and a breakdown of civil discourse. Additionally, the rise of social media has made it easier for misinformation to spread rapidly, further exacerbating the problem.

The author also explores the ways in which populist leaders have used media to their advantage, manipulating the public through fearmongering and divisive rhetoric. He argues that this trend poses a significant threat to democracy, as it undermines the principles of informed decision-making and civic engagement.

Ultimately, "The Revolution Will Be Televised" serves as a call to action for individuals to critically evaluate the sources of information they consume and to actively seek out diverse perspectives. By doing so, the author believes that we can combat the rise of populism and ensure the health of our democratic institutions.

In which countries are we anticipating a potential revolution? Can you provide a list of these countries and explain why?

1. Venezuela - ongoing political and economic crisis, widespread corruption and human rights abuses, potential for a coup or popular uprising
2. Iran - discontent with the government, economic hardships, human rights violations, potential for protests and revolution
3. Syria - ongoing civil war, political instability, sectarian tensions, potential for further unrest and revolution
4. Nigeria - corruption, poverty, ethnic and religious tensions, potential for social unrest and revolution
5. North Korea - oppressive regime, human rights abuses, potential for uprising and revolution
6. Saudi Arabia - discontent with the government, lack of political freedoms, economic challenges, potential for revolution
7. Yemen - ongoing civil war, humanitarian crisis, political instability, potential for revolution
8. Egypt - political repression, economic challenges, social unrest, potential for another revolution
9. Sudan - political instability, economic hardships, human rights abuses, potential for revolution

10. Algeria - dissatisfaction with the government, corruption, economic struggles, potential for revolution
11. Iraq - political instability, sectarian tensions, economic challenges, potential for revolution
12. Zimbabwe - political repression, economic hardships, lack of democracy, potential for revolution
13. Myanmar - ethnic and religious tensions, human rights abuses, potential for revolution
14. Afghanistan - ongoing conflict, political instability, economic challenges, potential for revolution
15. Pakistan - political corruption, economic struggles, social unrest, potential for revolution
16. Haiti - political corruption, poverty, lack of basic services, potential for revolution
17. Lebanon - political gridlock, economic crisis, sectarian tensions, potential for revolution
18. Bolivia - political turmoil, allegations of fraud, economic challenges, potential for revolution
19. Thailand - political unrest, military control, lack of democracy, potential for revolution
1. Turkey - authoritarian rule, crackdown on dissent, economic challenges, potential for revolution
2. India - religious and ethnic tensions, economic disparities, political corruption, potential for revolution
3. Bangladesh - political turmoil, human rights abuses, economic struggles, potential for revolution
4. Philippines - authoritarian rule, human rights violations, economic disparities, potential for revolution
5. Venezuela - ongoing political and economic crisis, widespread corruption and human rights abuses, potential for a coup or popular uprising
6. Ukraine - ongoing conflict with Russia, political corruption, economic challenges, potential for revolution
7. Belarus - authoritarian rule, lack of democracy, economic struggles, potential for revolution

8. Hong Kong - protests against Chinese control, lack of democracy, human rights abuses, potential for revolution
9. Colombia - ongoing conflict with guerrilla groups, political corruption, economic challenges, potential for revolution
10. Mexico - drug cartel violence, political corruption, economic disparities, potential for revolution
11. Brazil - political corruption, economic struggles, social inequality, potential for revolution

The timing of a potential revolution in these countries is difficult to predict, as it depends on a variety of factors such as government responses to protests, economic conditions, and levels of popular discontent. However, ongoing social unrest and political instability in many of these countries suggest that the possibility of revolution is a real concern.

Understanding how a revolution can occur in a democratic country is valuable.

In a democratic country, a revolution is possible when a significant portion of the population becomes dissatisfied with the current government or ruling party and feels that their voices are not being heard through the normal channels of democracy. This dissatisfaction can be fueled by a variety of factors, such as widespread corruption, economic inequality, social injustice, or a lack of political representation.

A revolution in a democratic country typically begins with peaceful protests, demonstrations, and civil disobedience to demand change. If these peaceful efforts are met with repression or violence from the government, they can escalate into more intense forms of resistance, such as strikes, boycotts, or even armed rebellion.

In order for a revolution to succeed in a democratic country, it often requires widespread support from the population, including various social groups, political parties, and civil society organizations. It may also require the involvement of the military or other security forces, who may choose to either support the government or align themselves with the protesters.

Ultimately, a revolution in a democratic country can lead to the overthrow of the existing government and the establishment of a new political system or leadership. However, it is important to note that revolutions can be complex and messy processes, often resulting in violence, instability, and uncertainty about the future. Therefore, it is crucial for all parties involved to prioritize nonviolent means of resistance and negotiation in order to achieve lasting and meaningful change.

Here are 10 examples of peaceful revolutions beginning with Gandhi.

1. The Salt March led by Mahatma Gandhi in 1930 in India, protesting against British colonial rule.
2. The Civil Rights Movement in the United States, led by figures such as Martin Luther King Jr., advocating for equal rights for African Americans.
3. The Velvet Revolution in Czechoslovakia in 1989, peacefully overthrowing the communist government.

4. The Orange Revolution in Ukraine in 2004, protesting against electoral fraud and advocating for fair elections.
5. The Arab Spring in 2010-2012, a series of anti-government protests and uprisings in various Middle Eastern countries.
6. The Umbrella Movement in Hong Kong in 2014, advocating for greater democracy and autonomy from China.
7. The Cedar Revolution in Lebanon in 2005, calling for the withdrawal of Syrian troops from the country.
8. The Velvet Divorce in Czechoslovakia in 1992, peacefully splitting the country into the Czech Republic and Slovakia.
9. The Rose Revolution in Georgia in 2003, peacefully overthrowing the government and advocating for democratic reforms.
10. The People Power Revolution in the Philippines in 1986, overthrowing the dictator Ferdinand Marcos and installing a democratic government.

The influence of mass media and social media in reporting on events happening around the clock and its effect on global public perception.

Mass media and social media play a crucial role in covering Life 24/7 events, providing real-time updates, news, and information to the global audience. The coverage of such events by mass media outlets such as news channels, newspapers, and online platforms helps to bring awareness to important issues, events, and developments happening around the world.

Social media platforms also play a significant role in covering Life 24/7 events, as they allow for instant communication and sharing of information among users. Social media users can share their own experiences, photos, and videos of events, providing a more personal and unfiltered perspective on what is happening.

The coverage of Life 24/7 events by mass media and social media can have a significant impact on global opinion. By providing up-to-date and accurate information, these platforms can shape public perception and understanding of events, influencing how people view and react to them.

For example, coverage of natural disasters, political unrest, or humanitarian crises can lead to increased awareness and support from the global community, prompting action and aid to those in need. On the other hand, biased or inaccurate coverage of events can distort the truth and create misinformation, leading to misunderstandings and potentially harmful consequences.

In conclusion, the pivotal role of mass media and social media in covering Life 24/7 events cannot be overstated. These platforms play a crucial role in shaping global opinion and raising awareness about critical issues. It is imperative for them to deliver accurate, unbiased, and timely information to ensure that the public is well-informed and empowered to make decisions based on facts. Let's work together to ensure that these platforms uphold their responsibility in providing reliable information to the masses.

Printed in Great Britain
by Amazon